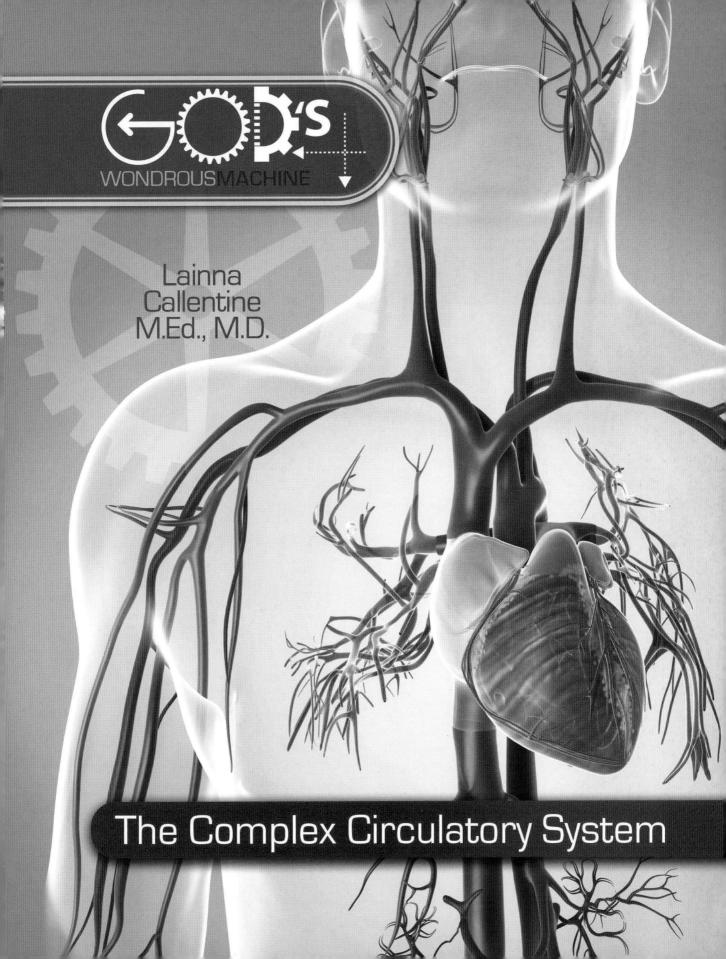

GOD'S
WONDROUS MACHINE

Lainna
Callentine
M.Ed., M.D.

The Complex Circulatory System

First printing: April 2016
Second printing: November 2019

Master Books®, P.O. Box 726,
Green Forest, AR 72638

Master Books® is a division of the
New Leaf Publishing Group, Inc.

ISBN: 978-0-89051-908-0
ISBN: 978-1-61458-487-2 (digital)
Library of Congress Number: 2015960972

Cover and Interior Design by Diana Bogardus

Unless otherwise noted, Scripture quotations are from the New International Version of the Bible.

Please consider requesting that a copy of this volume be purchased by your local library system.

Printed in China

Please visit our website for other great titles:
www.masterbooks.com

For information regarding author interviews, please contact the publicity department at (870) 438-5288.

Master Books®
A Division of New Leaf Publishing Group
www.masterbooks.com

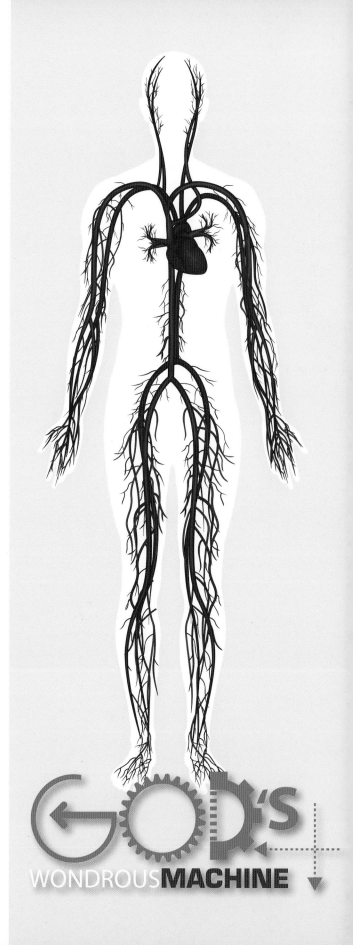

GOD'S
WONDROUS MACHINE

TABLE OF CONTENTS

How to Use This Book (All about Us!)

About this *God's Wondrous Machine* series:

Developed by a master's-trained teacher and homeschooling mother who happens to be a pediatrician, this is the third book in an innovative anatomy curriculum that focuses on the human body's circulatory system. It will create engaging opportunities for children to discover the wonders and workings of the human body.

Each book in this series delves into one of the major systems of the body; the first three of this nine-book series under development include the following:

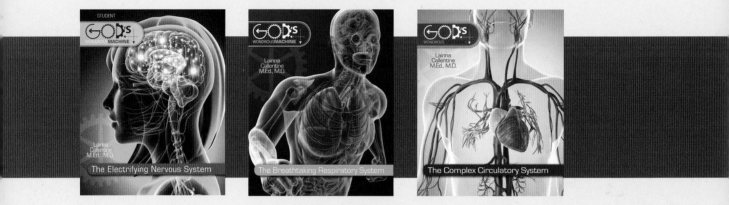

This book series is bursting with vibrantly colorful images, interesting historical and weird facts, anatomy, physiology, and modern innovations. You will engage your senses and have a multitude of choices for hands-on exploration. You will discover aspects of the human body from a doctor's perspective. Each book will focus on a particular system of the body, discussing how it works and how it doesn't at times. Common questions kids ask are answered to stimulate curiosity, and your senses will be engaged as the world of medicine is demystified.

This series gives many perspectives in science education by connecting to other fields of study (i.e., history, sociology, psychology, and theology), and it encourages the reader to appreciate God's magnificent handiwork: your body.

God's Wondrous Machine series recognizes that every learner is not the same. Whether used in a homeschool or classroom setting, the series' hands-on activities are based on the educational theory of Multiple Intelligence by Howard Gardner (which states there are many types of intelligences and recognizes different learning styles: musical–rhythmic, visual–spatial, verbal–linguistic, logical–mathematical, bodily–kinesthetic, interpersonal, intrapersonal, and naturalistic). It is flexible enough for endless customization for the skills, interests, and abilities of each student.

Using the Teacher Guide

This developing nine-book series will challenge the child in all facets of multiple intelligence. The parent/instructor is able to choose and customize hands-on activities that engage a multitude of learning styles and challenge the student to explore life's big issues. The program is specially designed for lower and upper elementary level students, including advanced learners with middle school proficiency!

You can use this book as an interesting:

▸ Unit Study

▸ Curriculum

▸ Supplemental Resource

An associated teacher guide is available. It contains perforated sheets for worksheets, and tests, in addition to a flexible educational calendar. This additional material allows for a multiple array of assessments for the instructor (i.e., project based, traditional testing, or portfolio assessment). It is designed to maximize the learning opportunities and retention of information from the book, as kids have fun learning about the mechanics and mysteries for themselves!

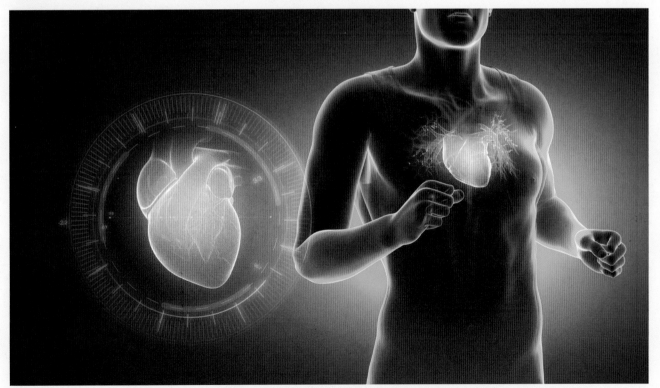

Exercise is important! Running can help stimulate muscles and help make the heart pump more efficiently. Doctors can check your heart by using a stethoscope, a device invented in 1816 by a young French physician who was embarrassed to place his ear to the chest of a young female patient, which at the time was the standard way to check someone's heartbeat.

About the Author

Dr. Lainna Callentine has a passion for science. She spent many hours as a child turning over rocks and wading through streams chasing tadpoles. She is from a family of six children. Her parents felt that education was a powerful tool. They instilled in her and her siblings a great love for learning.

Dr. Callentine wears many hats. She is a coach, teacher, pediatrician, and homeschool mother. She obtained her bachelor's degree in human development and social policy from Northwestern University in the school of education while competing as a full-scholarship athlete. She began her professional career as an elementary school teacher. She obtained her master's degree in education from Widener University. Then she went on to pursue her lifelong dream of becoming a doctor. Dr. Callentine obtained her medical degree from University of Illinois College of Medicine. She worked in one of the busiest emergency rooms in Illinois before answering the call to go home and homeschool her children.

She founded Sciexperience and travels nationally as a speaker doing inspiring hands-on science workshops for all ages. She continues to utilize her medical training as a missionary doctor in a clinic for the uninsured. She is an adjunct professor at Wheaton College as an instructor of clinical kinesiology. She is a member of the Christian Medical and Dental Society. She enjoys basketball, time with her husband and three kids, and the outdoors.

Web information:

www.sciexperience.com

Facebook page: www.facebook.com/GodsWon-drousMachine

LinkedIn: www.linkedin.com/pub/lainna-callentine-m-ed-m-d/50/744/a0b/

A Note from the Author

Wow! Congratulations! You are actually reading "A Note from the Author" page! Really? Who really reads these anyway? I have a sad confession — when I was a kid I would always skip this section. "Who cares?" I would say. "This is not assigned, and I certainly won't be tested on this."

I am glad you stopped by to spend some "quality" time prior to digging into *The Complex Circulatory System*. I am blown away by the complexity of life. This is not a random sequence of events. Design is everywhere.

My prayer for you is to continue to grow in the love of Christ. I am absolutely sure that God has big plans for your life. You are His wondrous creation. My hope is that this book as well as the other books in this series of God's Wondrous Machine will draw you to the Great Designer. You are deeply loved by your Heavenly Father. There are many distractions and arguments about this design, as well as the time period that God created it. Make no mistake, God's Word is true. This is a battle for souls. May you walk boldly and heed His call.

In His Service,

Dr. Lainna Callentine

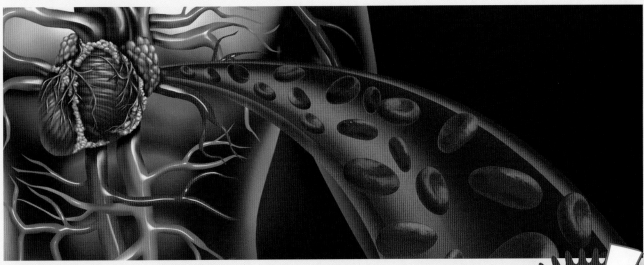

Dedication

To my dear family, thanks for standing by my side.

D.R., my best friend, thanks for your steadfast love and unending encouragement. You have been there in sickness and health.

My children: Michael, Jay, and Hannah, where does time go? Thank you for your support and love.

Your blood travels 12,000 miles throughout your body each day. That is the same distance basically as travelling across the United States four times!

I AM wonderfully made

VOCABULARY LEVELS

Choose the word list based on your skill level. Every student should be able to master Level 1 words. Add words from Levels 2 and 3 as needed. More proficient students should be able to learn all three levels.

Level 1 Vocabulary

- Anemia
- Aorta
- Arteries
- Arterioles
- Atrium
- Bone marrow
- Closed circulatory system
- Fetus
- Hemoglobin
- Open circulatory system
- Prothrombin
- Red Blood Cells
- Stethoscope
- Valves
- Veins
- White blood cells

Level 2 Vocabulary

Review and Know Level 1 Vocabulary

- Antibodies
- Antigens
- Buffy coat
- Capillary
- Coronary
- Epicardium
- Erythrocytes
- Hematophagic
- Hemophilia
- Hemostasis
- Malaria
- Myocardium
- Pericardial sac
- Platelets
- Sickle cell anemia
- Stem cell
- Syncope
- Systole
- Tachycardia
- Universal donor
- Universal receiver
- Ventricles

Level 3 Vocabulary

Review and Know Level 1 and 2 Vocabulary

- Auscultate
- Bradycardia
- Centrifuge
- Chordae tendineae
- Diastole
- Electrocardiogram
- Endocardium
- Hematopoiesis
- Myocardial infarction
- Prothrombin
- Sinoatrial node
- Tricuspid valve
- Venules

See It, Say It, Know It!

Word [Pronunciation]	Definition
Anemia [ah-ne´me-ah]	A problem with the blood in which oxygen delivered to the organs and tissues is decreased. It can be a symptom of many different diseases.
Antibodies [an-ti-bod-eez]	Blood proteins that are made to attack a specific invader, like bacteria or viruses. They set off a cascade of events to assist the body in a stronger defense.
Antigens [an´tĭ-jenz]	A foreign substance, like bacteria or virus, that triggers an immune response and causes antibodies to spring into action.
Aorta [a-or´tah]	The largest artery in the body that originates from the left ventricle and sends oxygenated blood to the body.
Arteries [ahr´ter-ez]	Vessels that carry oxygenated blood from the heart to the body.
Arterioles [ahr-te´re-ōlz]	Small vessels that carry oxygenated blood that connects to capillaries.
Atrium [a´tre-um]	The upper chambers of the heart in which blood enters the heart. There are two atrium, the right and left atriums.
Auscultate [ô´skəl-tāt´]	To listen; to listen to the sounds of the body.
Bradycardia [brady-car-dia]	A slow heartbeat that is typically less than 60 beats a minute for an adult.
Bone marrow [bohn mar´o]	The soft, spongy material in the middle of bones.
Buffy coat [bufé kōt]	When blood is centrifuged, spun in a test tube in a machine, the blood separates into three parts. This middle part is composed of white blood cells and platelets
Capillary [kap´ĭ-lar˝e]	Smallest arterial blood vessel; connects the arterioles with the venules.
Centrifuge [cen´trĭ-fūj]	To spin around; a machine used to spin test tubes of blood at high speeds in order to cause the parts of blood to separate.
Closed circulatory system	A blood system composed of vessels of different sizes that encloses the blood at all times. The blood is pumped by the heart and does not fill body cavities.
Chordae tendineae [kor´dah ten di nee a]	Fibrous strings that connect to the edges of the heart valves. They keep the valves from inverting or flipping backwards. Also known as the "heart strings."

9

Word [Pronunciation]	Definition
Coronary [kôr´ə-nĕr´ē,]	The blood vessels that line the outside of the heart.
Diastole [dī-ăs´tə-lē]	The phase in the heartbeat when the heart muscle relaxes and allows the heart chambers to fill with blood.
Electrocardiogram [ĭ-lĕk´trō-kär´dē-ə-grăm´]	A machine that graphically records the heart's electrical activity.
Endocardium [ĕn´dō-kär´dē-əm]	The inner muscle layer of the heart; the muscle that lines the inside of the heart.
Epicardium [ĕp´ĭ-kär´dē-əm]	The outer muscle layer of the heart that lies under the pericardial sac.
Erythrocytes [ē•rith•rō•sits]	A red blood cell that contains hemoglobin and transports oxygen.
Fetus [fē´təs]	An unborn baby.
Hematophagic [hĕ´mă-tō-fă´jē-ă]	The act of an animal or insect like a mosquito drinking blood.
Hematopoiesis [he″mah-to-poi-e´sis]	The formation of blood cells. In the fetus, it takes place at sites including the liver, spleen, and thymus. From birth throughout the rest of life, it is mainly in the bone marrow.
Hemoglobin [he´mo-glo″bin]	A protein housed in red blood cells that contain iron. Hemoglobin facilitates in carrying oxygen.
Hemophilia [hee-muh-fil-ee-uh]	Any of several X-linked genetic disorders transmitted from the mother's genes, is a disease that occurs mainly in males. Excessive bleeding occurs due to the absence or abnormality of a clotting factor in the blood.
Hemostasis [he″mo-sta´sis]	Stopping the escape of blood by natural means (either clot formation or vessel spasm).
Malaria [muh-lair-ee-uh]	A disease transmitted by mosquitos in which a parasite infects the red blood cells; can be deadly.
Myocardial infarction [mi″o-kahr´de-al in-fark´ shun]	A heart attack.
Myocardium [mi″o-kar´de-um]	The middle and thickest layer of the heart wall muscle.
Open circulatory system	System in which the blood is pumped by the heart and fills the body cavities. The blood does not stay within the vessels.

	Level 1 Vocabulary
	Level 2 Vocabulary
	Level 3 Vocabulary

Word [Pronunciation]	Definition
Pericardial sac [per″ĭ-kahr′de-al sak]	Fibrous double-layered sac that surrounds the heart. It is filled with a lubricant that allows the heart to move without friction.
Platelets [plat′lits]	Small cells in the blood that are important in hemostasis, forming blood clots.
Prothrombin [pro-throm′bin]	A clotting factor, made in the liver, that is in the blood. It is activated to thrombin for clot formation.
Red blood cells	Cells in the blood that contain hemoglobin, an iron that carries oxygen.
Sickle cell anemia [ah-ne′me-ah]	A blood disease that is inherited in which the red blood cells become misshaped to a sickle-like appearance. Causes long-term problems.
Sinoatrial node [sahy-noh-ey-tree-uh]	A mass of muscle tissue on the top of the right atrium that is the electrical pacemaker of the heart.
Stem cell	A cell that has the ability to differentiate to other specialized cells.
Stethoscope [steth′o-skōp]	A medical device used to listen and magnify the sounds heard in the body.
Syncope [sing′kah-pe]	To lose consciousness; pass out.
Systole [sis′to-le]	The phase in the heart cycle of beating in which the heart chambers contract to expel blood out of the heart.
Tachycardia [tak″e-kahr′de-ah]	A fast heartbeat that typically is over 100 beats a minute in an adult.
Tricuspid valve	The heart valve between the right atrium and right ventricle.
Universal donor	A person who has type O blood.
Universal receiver	A person who has type AB blood.
Valves [valv]	The "door" between the chambers of the heart that prevents blood from flowing backwards.
Veins [vān]	Blood vessels in the body that carry deoxygenated blood. They transport blood to the heart.
Ventricles [ven′trĭ-k'l]	The lower chambers of the heart.
Venules [ven′ūl]	Small blood vessels that carry deoxygenated blood toward the heart. They connect the capillaries to the veins.
White blood cells	Blood cells that are part of the immune system that fight invaders that attack the body.

*Pronunciation Keys from http://medical-dictionary.thefreedictionary.com

Lightning flashed. The cloud hurled its pellets downward. A blood-curdling scream resonated through the cold, dank, and dreary marble halls . . . a suspenseful way to begin a book on *The Complex Circulatory System,* right? Just the mention of the word or seeing blood causes some people to feel woozy and go wobbly in the knees. Some people will even pass out at the very sight of blood. Take heart. There will be no need to be faint of heart.

Our heart beats passionately. It never stops. It never rests. It works around the clock, day and night. It starts to beat after you were conceived in your mother's womb at 3 to 4 weeks (a full-term pregnancy is 40 weeks), and continues until the day God calls you heavenward. Aside from our Heavenly Father, Lord, God, and Jesus, no two words are more heavily mentioned in the Bible than "blood" and "heart." The word blood is mentioned in the Bible over 400 times. Heart is mentioned over a staggering 900 times. We will take a look at some of the powerful images illustrated and represented by these words.

The Complex Circulatory System will catapult you into a whole new dimension. First, we will take an historical excursion through the pages of time and see how our knowledge of the circulatory system has expanded. We will learn all about blood, where it comes from, and how clots develop. Next, we will wade through the life-giving fluid that courses through the highways of your body. We will explore bloodsucking critters and enter the atrium of the heart and peer into the heart's many rooms. My prayer is that as we journey through the tributaries of your body, you will gain a deeper understanding of the magnificent artistry God has fashioned in you.

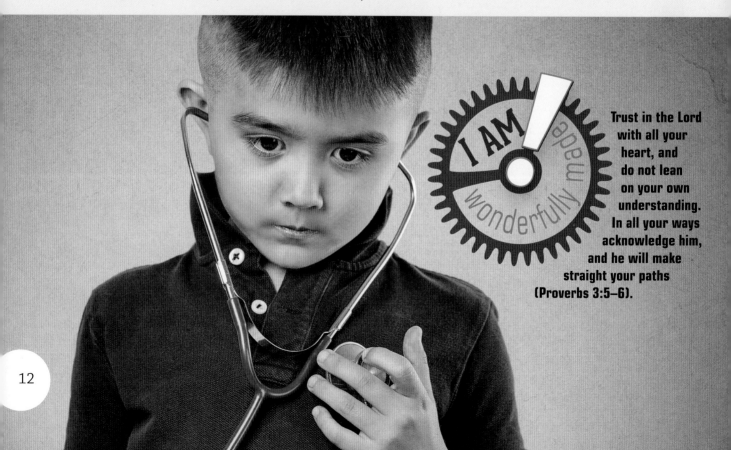

I AM **!** wonderfully made

Trust in the Lord with all your heart, and do not lean on your own understanding. In all your ways acknowledge him, and he will make straight your paths (Proverbs 3:5–6).

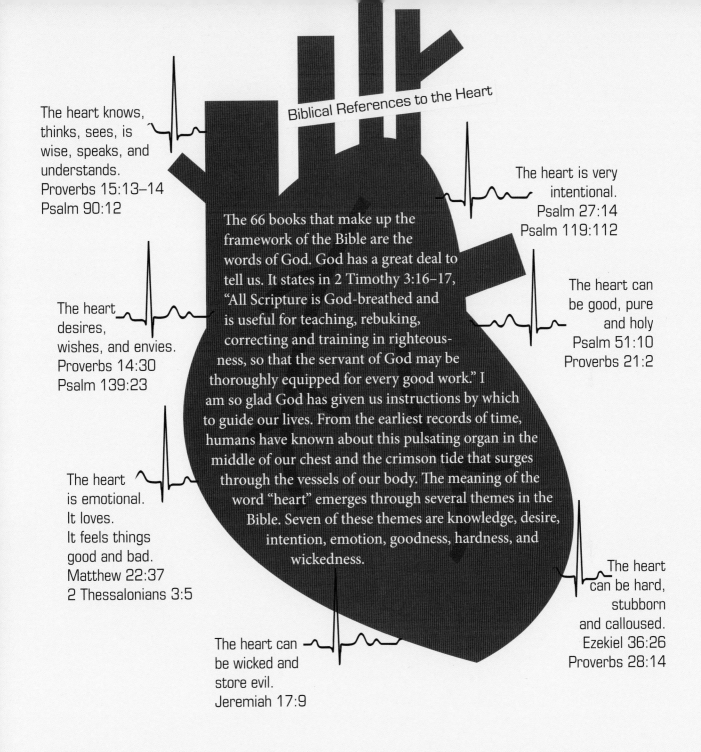

The heart knows, thinks, sees, is wise, speaks, and understands.
Proverbs 15:13–14
Psalm 90:12

The heart is very intentional.
Psalm 27:14
Psalm 119:112

The heart desires, wishes, and envies.
Proverbs 14:30
Psalm 139:23

The heart can be good, pure and holy
Psalm 51:10
Proverbs 21:2

The heart is emotional. It loves. It feels things good and bad.
Matthew 22:37
2 Thessalonians 3:5

The heart can be hard, stubborn and calloused.
Ezekiel 36:26
Proverbs 28:14

The heart can be wicked and store evil.
Jeremiah 17:9

The 66 books that make up the framework of the Bible are the words of God. God has a great deal to tell us. It states in 2 Timothy 3:16–17, "All Scripture is God-breathed and is useful for teaching, rebuking, correcting and training in righteousness, so that the servant of God may be thoroughly equipped for every good work." I am so glad God has given us instructions by which to guide our lives. From the earliest records of time, humans have known about this pulsating organ in the middle of our chest and the crimson tide that surges through the vessels of our body. The meaning of the word "heart" emerges through several themes in the Bible. Seven of these themes are knowledge, desire, intention, emotion, goodness, hardness, and wickedness.

It has taken us many generations to acquire the understanding of the heart in the context of our biological processes. Our Lord amazes me. Before man made these "great" discoveries, God's creation and order already existed. We have just begun to understand some of the complexities of His handiwork, to put words and descriptions to this order. We continue to gain increasing understanding of this order. Never will our understanding and intellect put us on equal footing with our Lord. May our hearts become tender to the soothing words and guidance of our Heavenly Father.

Any time when we peek back at the timelines of history, it is important to remember that it is an account of the past. People's accounts can differ depending on that particular person's perspective. The context in which an historical event occurs is important to take in consideration. Context is the circumstances or situation in which something happens. These discoveries did not happen inside an airless and weightless vacuum. Our progress in science builds on our prior knowledge. Each intellectual discovery provides a foothold to reach up to further our understanding. Scientific reasoning can be very delicate and at times silenced depending on a person's or culture's worldview. We will take a look at this as we tour the historical timeline of the circulatory system.

We begin in the year 384 B.C. with Aristotle who was born in Macedonia. He was a Greek philosopher and scientist. He believed the heart was the center of a person. The heart was where the soul dwelled and was where blood was manufactured in the body. In 340 B.C., Praxagoras was the first to differentiate between arteries and veins. He believed that the arteries had their origin in the heart and carried "pneuma." Pneuma has its origins in Greek. It means to "breathe" and is related to the "spirit" and the "soul" in the religious context. Arteries were full of "spiritual" air. Erasistratus, a Greek anatomist (one who studies the body) and royal physician, described the heart as being a pump. He also in 250s B.C. saw the heart as a source of both arteries and veins. This was the wisdom of the times. This set the stage for one of the most influential physicians of the middle ages. Claudius Galenus, was born in Pergamum, Asia Minor (Western Turkey), during the peak of the Roman Empire in the approximate year of A.D.

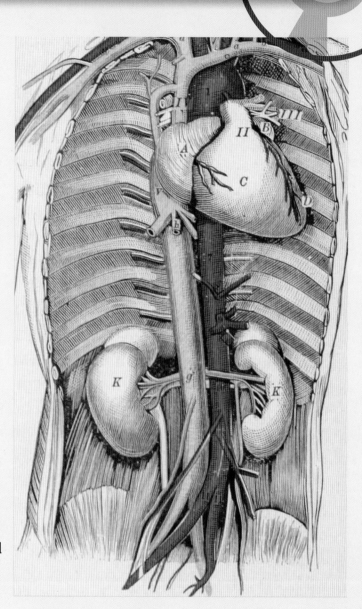

129. He was better known as Galen. Galen left an indelible mark on the anatomical world. So deep was his impact that his view of the circulatory system was believed for 15 centuries!

Word Wise!

TOURNIQUET is any device that uses pressure to stop the flow of blood, usually through the arteries of an arm or leg, as after a serious injury.

If you lived in these times you would believe the following about the body:

The body's function was to refine the food you ate. Natural spirits had their beginnings in the food and drink you consumed. Vital spirits were derived from the air. Veins carried natural spirits. Arteries carried vital spirits.

Food was transformed in the liver. Veins originated at the liver. These veins contained the four humors or liquids of the body: yellow and black bile, blood, and phlegm. The blood of the veins went to the heart, and air and blood mixed in the left side of the heart. The heart was like a burning cauldron that produced heat and provided body warmth. (The brain cooled the body.) The humors naturally flowed around the body and went only where they were needed. The blood was consumed.

Why was this view so important? This theory guided the ideas about the origin of disease. Illness and disease were seen as functions of an imbalance of humors or a shift in its flow in the body. Treatment was aimed at restoration of this natural balance. Bloodletting was the practice of bleeding someone to restore this "healthy" balance. (We will talk a bit more about this later.) Tourniquets, which stop blood flow in an artery or vein, were also applied to parts of the body in attempts to redirect the flow of blood to other areas of the body. Today, we only use tourniquets in emergency situations to stop the bleeding from a wound.

Galen began his study of medicine at the age of 16. At the age of 28, he was appointed to the post of surgeon to the gladiators. He received a great deal of on-the-job training patching up wounded gladiators. In the year A.D. 162, he became the leading authority on medical knowledge and was appointed to the position of physician to the emperor. Galen left the world a legacy of these essential views:

	Galen's View	Modern View
1.	Veins contained blood. These veins were open ended, and the blood bathed the organs.	Veins do in fact carry blood. They are not open ended or bathe the organs. They carry deoxygenated blood.
2.	A small amount of the blood provided nourishment to the lungs.	All the blood in the body is transported to the lungs to obtain oxygen.
3.	The heart pulsated.	The heart does beat and therefore it could be considered to "pulsate."
4.	Breathing cooled the heated body and yielded the vital spirits.	Breathing is not the essential way that the body cools itself. "Vital" spirits are not taken up by the lungs.
5.	Arteries contained air and blood.	Arteries do contain blood. Oxygen is dissolved in the blood and is transported on hemoglobin in the red blood cells.
6.	Arteries were located deep in the body and pulsated. The blood in the arteries was hotter, thinner, and more "spirituous." Veins were located close to the surface.	Arteries can lay deep and superficially in the body. They do pulsate with each beat of the heart.
7.	The whole body breathes in and out.	The lungs do the breathing.

This accepted view of the body did not advance for nearly 15 centuries. History and science discovery was guided by the worldview of the times. Over the course of these 15 centuries, the Roman Catholic Church dominated the attitudes and direction of the world of medicine. In essence, anyone who disagreed with the established church was labeled a heretic and was severally punished. A heretic is someone who dissents or disagrees from the established views or what is thought as the revealed truth. Illness was seen strictly as punishment from God. Today we have a process called the scientific method in which one asks questions, develops a hypothesis, and tests this hypothesis through experimentation. During this time, there was no tradition in the way scientific knowledge was acquired. People feared testing commonly held beliefs proposed by Galen. They also feared the church. It wasn't until the Reformation, among other events, when Martin Luther on October 31, 1517, nailed his *95 Theses* on the door of the All Saints' Church in Wittenberg. He challenged the church. The two over-arching points of his theses were that the Bible was the center of religious authority and that we reach salvation by our faith and not just by our deeds.

Fast forward hundreds of years to modern times, and we still have a battle of worldviews. Faith and belief in the Bible do not suppress scientific ideas and advancement. In fact, they are supported more and more with each new discovery, which furthers us to magnify the great designer in our Heavenly Father.

Galen's open-ended vascular system

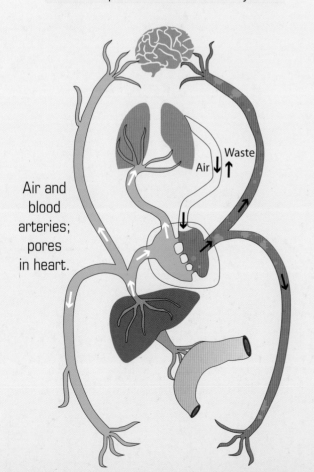

Air and blood arteries; pores in heart.

Air Waste

Harvey's closed circulatory system

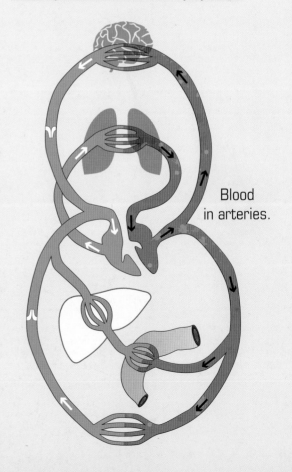

Blood in arteries.

16

This symbol for the barber's pole began during the Dark Ages; the red represented the bloody bandages wrapped around a pole. Early versions had a brass wash basin on the top and bottom. The top basin was a representation of where the leeches were kept. The bottom one was the symbol for the basin used to collect the blood. The staff was the item that a patient would grasp to encourage the flow of blood after a bloodletting procedure.

2000 B.C. to A.D. 1500

Mayan kings and queens who ruled in Central America would open their own veins so that their blood could be used in ceremonies.

460-370 B.C.

Ancient Greek doctor Hippocrates (460–370 B.C.), was considered the father of medicine. He is credited with the idea of the four humors.

335 B.C.

Herophilus (335–280 B.C.), a Greek doctor, was considered to be the father of anatomy.

129-200

Claudius Galen of Pergamon (129–200) operated on gladiators. He greatly influenced the understanding of medicine and anatomy in the middle ages based on Hippocrates theory of the four humors.

410-1095

In medieval times, barbers were also surgeons. Doctors of the time considered surgery messy and beneath them. Barbers were good with a sharp blade, not only could they cut hair, but they would practice procedures from bloodletting to amputation of limbs. The barber pole was originally red and white striped.

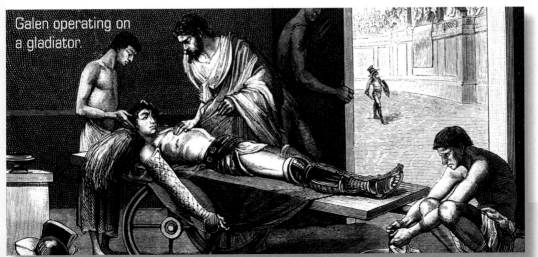

Galen operating on a gladiator.

17

1500

1553

1543

1578

1666

Leonardo Da Vinci (1452–1519) noted tiny "hairs" in tissues. He was interested in the link between form and action of the body. He made the first accurate drawing of the body as well as the heart and its valves.

Michael Servetus (1511?–1553) was a theologian and physician who was burned at the stake. He was considered a heretic for his description of the circulation of the blood through the lungs.

Andreas Vesalius (1514–1564) wrote one of the first books on the human anatomy entitled *De Humani Corporis Fabrica (On the Fabric of the Human Body)*.

William Harvey (1578–1657), an English physician, was the first to describe blood circulation in the body. He stated that blood flowed in a closed circuit — it was conserved, which means that the blood was not consumed by the organs. His discovery caused him much concern because it went against centuries of medical thought. He said, "Not only do I fear danger to myself from malice of a few, but I dread lest I have all men as enemies."

Richard Lower (1631–1691), a physician, followed the works of William Harvey. He pioneered the idea of blood transfusions. He experimented on transfusing dogs. He even transfused a lamb's blood into a human — but such practices were very dangerous so laws in both England and France were created to stop it!

Lower transfusing blood into a man's arm from a lamb.

1670

1799

1818

1823

1832

Marcello Malpighi of Bologna (1628–1691), a biologist and physician, utilized a primitive microscope and discovered a network of tiny vessels called capillaries in the lung of a frog. This discovery linked the arteries and veins.

George Washington (1732–1799) died due to bloodletting. After a day of riding his horse out in the cold, he returned to find his throat sore. Soreness and the swelling in his throat advanced. He became short of breath, and a team of doctors were called. They utilized the most "effective" treatment of the times, bloodletting. It is said nearly 40 percent of his blood volume was removed, and he died. Before dying, George Washington thanked the doctors for their excellent care.

James Blundell (1791–1878) became the first in the United States to perform a successful blood transfusion. The transfusion was performed on a woman who had just delivered a baby. She immediately suffered from severe bleeding. He took 4 ounces from the woman's husband and transfused it into her. Today we know it's not that simple. People have one of four different types of blood, and it can be deadly if you receive the wrong kind during a transfusion.

The first medical journal, *The Lancet,* was published. *The Lancet* still exists today. It is one of the leading medical journals. Thomas Wakley (1792–1862) first published it on October 5, 1823. As the journal was going to press he stated, "A lancet can be an arched window to let in the light or it can be a sharp surgical instrument to cut out the dross and I intend to use it in both senses." A lancet was the indispensable tool utilized in bloodletting. It was used to cut the skin and blood vessels.

The laws were changed, and medical professionals could legally use donated bodies for study and dissection.

The picture above is Rembrandt van Rijn's *The Anatomy Lesson of Dr. Nicolaes Tulp,* completed in 1632. Dissection was not limited to the eager learning eyes of apprentice doctors of the day; dissections were also held for public "amusement." You could even buy tickets for these events.

1893

1896

1903

1900's

1919

Daniel Hale Williams (1856–1931) was an African American general surgeon who performed the first successful open heart surgery and founded the first non-segregated hospital in the United States. He operated on James Cornish at Provident Hospital in Chicago. Mr. Cornish had been stabbed in the heart. Today's common practice of blood transfusion and the use of blood products was not safely utilized at that time. Even without this life-saving practice, he was able to suture (sew) the covering around Cornish's heart, saving his life.

Ernest Henry Starling (1866–1927), an English physiologist (a person who studies the body's processes), was the first to explain the maintenance of a fluid balance in the body. It is called Starling's Law. The law states that the stroke volume (the amount of blood pumped into the left ventricle per a heartbeat) of the heart will increase with additional blood filling into the ventricle. The more the heart wall stretches due to increased blood flow, the more force the heart muscle will use to contract.

Willem Einthoven (1860–1927) was a Dutch doctor and physiologist who invented the first electrocardiogram (EKG or ECG). It was already understood and accepted in medicine that the heart generated electrical activity. However, prior to Einthoven's invention, the only way to record this activity was placing electrodes directly on the heart muscle. This was impractical. He won the Nobel Prize in Physiology or Medicine in 1924.

Karl Landsteiner (1868–1943) an Austrian-born biologist and physician was the first to identify the major blood groups: A, B, AB, and O. He discovered that agglutinins were found on blood red blood cells that caused an immune reaction in which blood clumps when two different types of blood are mixed.

Jules Bordet (1870–1961), physician, was awarded the Nobel Prize in Physiology or Medicine for his discovery of factors in blood that destroy bacteria and how the blood breaks apart (called hemolysis) due to foreign blood cells in the body.

20

1920s	**1930s**	**1944**	**1952**	**1967**

Werner Forssmann (1904–1979), a physician born in Berlin, used himself as a test subject to prove the medical procedure for cardiac catherization was possible. He inserted a catheter, a type of tube, threading it into a vein at the fold of his arm and pushed the tube deeper and deeper until the top was inside the right side of his heart. With the tube still in, he went to the hospital radiology department and took x-rays to confirm his findings. He was awarded the Noble Prize in Physiology or Medicine in 1956.

Charles Richard Drew (1904–1950), was an African American physician and surgeon who is credited for blood banks. He studied how blood transfusions were given, and invented better techniques for storing blood. During World War II, he utilized this new knowledge to help provide life-saving blood storage to help wounded soldiers in the field.

Helen Brooke Taussig (1898–1986), physician, is credited with being the founder of pediatric cardiology. She assisted in the development of the Blalock-Taussig Shunt. This is a surgical procedure that helps children born with heart defects, "blue baby syndrome," that cause them to be blue. She was awarded the Medal of Freedom from President Lyndon Johnson. In 1965, she became the first woman president of the American Heart Association.

Michael DeBakey (1908–2008) invented a new kind of graft for repairing torn arteries. In 1932, he invented a part for the first heart-lung machines. These machines are utilized for heart surgery. He was the first person to identify the smoking of cigarettes as a connection to lung cancer. In the 1950s, the DeBakey Dacron Graft was used in repairing damaged blood vessels.

Christiaan N. Barnard (1922–2001), a South American cardiac surgeon, was a pioneer who performed the first successful human heart transplant. Although his patient lived only 21 days after, it was still considered a great success.

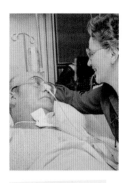

1982

1991

Barney Clark at 61 years of age survived a Jarvik-7 artificial heart for 112 days. Dr. William DeVries (1943–) performed the surgery. Clark knew that his chances for long-term survival were not likely, but he agreed to the heart to help further medicine.

Dr. Drew Gaffney (1946–), physician, flew on NASA's space shuttle as a "payload specialist." A payload specialist is someone who rides as an expert in a particular field. While on board, he studied how the heart and the circulatory system adapted to flight in space. This was the first mission to explore the human body in space. A catheter, a long tube, was inserted into his elbow prior to lift off and threaded to his heart. This allowed close measurement of his heart functions.

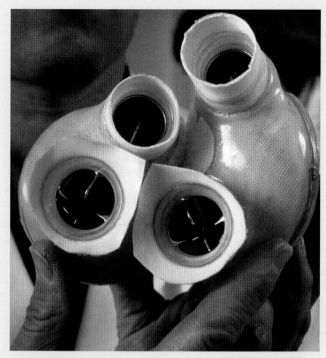

A number of artificial hearts were proposed and experimented with since the first one by Vladimir Demikhov in 1937, who transplanted it into a dog. There were limited successes in tests with animals, but this helped to advance understanding of the challenges. Here you can see the major blood vessels on the Jarvik-7, an aluminum and plastic artificial heart used during the first successful human implant in 1982 at the University of Utah Medical Centre in Salt Lake City. The Jarvik-7 heart relied on external power for compressed air and electricity. The patient had a six-foot lifeline to the support equipment.

Dr. Robert Jarvik, developer of the Jarvik-7 artificial heart, and Dr. William DeVries who, with Dr. Tom Kessler (not pictured), performed the first successful permanent artificial heart surgery.

The first total artificial heart implanted in a human body was developed by Domingo Liotta and placed by surgeon Dr. Denton Cooley in 1969 at St. Luke's Episcopal Hospital in Houston. (Dr. Liotta joined the staff at the hospital in Texas in 1961 as the director of the Artificial Heart Program. He was hired by Dr. Michael DeBakey.) The patient lived for sixty-four hours with the artificial heart pumping oxygenated blood through his body until a human heart could be available for transplant. The patient died soon after receiving a real heart, and there was criticism about the use of the Liotta-Cooley plastic heart. However, it did show how artificial hearts could be used until real hearts were donated.

Word Wise!

The HIPPOCRATIC OATH, named after Hippocrates, is an oath that doctors are required to swear upon upholding professional standards in practicing medicine and the care of the patients.

Our knowledge of medicine continues to march on.

Today, we are looking at new ways to diagnose heart disease much earlier. An item with great promise is the Computed Tomography Angiography or CTA. It helps to find small blocks in the arteries that surround the heart. A dye is injected in a vessel in a patient's arm. A special x-ray machine called a CT scanner takes images of the heart and the dye flowing through the blood vessels. It can show where blockage exists in the vessels.

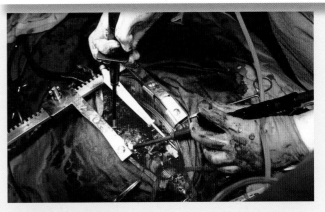

A new artificial blood is being tested in the United Kingdom. If successful, it could provide an answer to blood shortages. Perhaps it can be used in patients who refuse blood transfusion on the grounds of religious objection.

Maybe God has a plan for you to make contributions to the field of cardiology. He has given you unlimited potential. Walk boldly. Keep your eyes on Him. Look for ways to magnify His wonder.

we got the beat

Racial segregation existed in the United States and even existed in the donation of blood. Charles Richard Drew resigned from his position with the American Red Cross over this issue. The American Red Cross did not change its position on this policy of segregation until 1950.

Blood brothers, bad blood, blood oath, cold-blooded, blood-thirsty, blood bath and blood ties are just a few idioms that you may have encountered in reference to blood. An idiom is an expression that has a meaning that is not obvious from the traditional definition of the words used. Blood can have many colorful meanings.

In the Bible, three of the biggest themes central to blood are references to life, sacrifice, and salvation. In the Old Testament, animal sacrifice was a common practice. The best of the best animals were selected for the offering to God. The animals provided a way to atone, or make right, wrongdoings. In Exodus 12, blood from an unblemished lamb was placed on the top and the two sides of the door frame to protect the firstborn of the Israelites during the Passover. An angel passed through the lands of Egypt destroying the firstborn. Those that had marked their door frames with blood were protected. It was a curse that the pharaoh brought on himself and his land when he refused to release the Israelites from slavery.

The ultimate sacrifice was the blood Jesus shed for us on the Cross. During the Last Supper with His disciples in Mark 14:23–24 it states:

Then he took a cup, and when he had given thanks, he gave it to them, and they all drank from it. "This is my blood of the covenant, which is poured out for many," he said to them.

Functions of Blood

Blood is important. It has great significance in keeping us alive, not only spiritually but also physically. There is an average of 4–5 liters of blood in an adult. That is the total of 2 to 2½ two-liter bottles of soda pop.

Word Wise!

BLOOD is the liquid that flows through arteries and veins within the body. The word is related to blut in German, *blōd* in Old English, and *bloed* in Dutch.

24

What is the function of blood? Of course, we all know it is better for it to be in our body instead of flowing out of our body. Let's dig a bit deeper. Following are the functions of blood:

1.	Blood acts as a delivery man.	As the blood flows through the miles and miles of highways of blood vessels, it delivers gases like oxygen, nutrients, and hormones. These items are essential for our cells to work efficiently.
2.	Blood acts as a garbage man.	As the cells complete their multitude of biological activities, waste products are generated. The waste is transported out of the cells and thrown into the blood stream where it can be transported for disposal by our kidneys.
3.	Blood helps control the heat in our bodies.	When you go out for a run, your body heats up. You may notice that your skin may become red, sweaty, and flushed. The blood vessels under your skin dilate (become larger) to allow the heat to be more effectively released from your body. This helps you to cool off.
4.	Blood controls the pH balance in your body	pH is a number scale that rates the level of acid vs. base in a substance. Scratching your head, still not clear? Okay, let's look at it another way. Your body likes a pH of 7. This is considered in the middle of the road on the pH scale. (The scale has a range from 0-14.) If the value is higher than 7, the solution is considered in the basic range. The higher you go the more "basic" it is. Milk of Magnesia® has a basic pH and is a medicine that can help settle an upset stomach. Less than 7 is considered to be acidic. The lower the number, the more acidic it is. Lemon juice has a pH of 3. This gives it its sour taste. Your blood helps to keep the pH in a tight range because your body works best at a neutral level of 7.
5.	Blood is comprised of elements that protect us against blood loss.	There is a special chain of events that happens in the blood that helps you to form clots. This keeps us from bleeding excessively. We will look deeper into this shortly.
6.	Blood protects us from foreign invaders like bacteria and diseases.	There are special cells in the blood to help us fight infection.

we got the beat

It is interesting to note that if you ever were to have the unfortunate accident of knocking out a permanent tooth, it is recommended that the tooth be put in milk when you are in transport to the dentist. Milk is a substance that has a neutral pH of 7, just like your body.

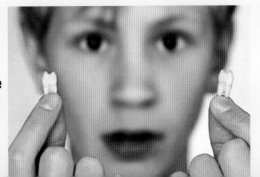

The Parts of Blood

Blood serves many functions. This versatile liquid has many components. These components assist in helping blood perform its many jobs. You may have had an experience in which you went to a lab or the hospital where they took a sample of your blood for testing. A small needle was inserted just under your skin into a vein. Your blood would have been collected in a clear tube. Once the blood was collected, it is placed in a machine called a centrifuge. The machine spins the blood around and around. This allows the components of the blood to separate from each other. Each component can be easily sampled and tested once separated.

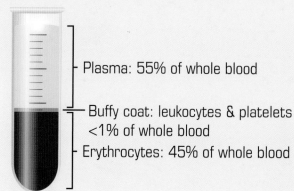

Plasma: 55% of whole blood

Buffy coat: leukocytes & platelets <1% of whole blood

Erythrocytes: 45% of whole blood

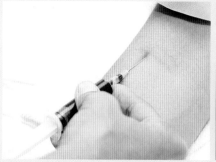

Withdraw blood and place in tube

Place tube in Centrifuge Machine

The machine spins the blood around to separate

Blood before spun in centrifuge machine

After separation, each component of the blood can be easily seen and tested.

Plasma

Three visual layers are seen after the blood is spun in the centrifuge. The top layer is a yellow straw-like color called plasma. Over half of your blood, 55 percent to be exact, is composed of plasma. Have you ever skinned your knee? After the bleeding stops, you may have noticed a clear to yellow watery substance oozing from your scraped knee. That is plasma!

Plasma is predominantly water. Dissolved in this watery substance are electrolytes like sodium, potassium, calcium, and others. Plasma also contains vital proteins like albumin (helps maintain a type of fluid pressure inside the vessels), fibrinogen (helps in clot formation) and globulins (there are many different types to help in processes like immunity). Plasma contains dissolved nutrients like sugar and vitamins as well as gases like oxygen and carbon dioxide.

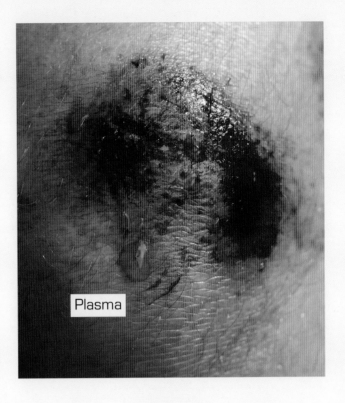

Plasma

Buffy Coat

Under the plasma level, you will find the buffy coat. When most grown-ups think of "buffy" coat they may think of the nice shiny, waxy coat given to their car to restore its luster. The buffy coat is only 1 percent of your blood. It contains your white blood cells (WBC) and platelets. The white blood cells are important in your immunity. They help you to fight illness and disease by producing antibodies, special biological heat-seeking missiles that are launched to attack unwelcome guests in your body.

Platelets contribute to the process of hemostasis. Whew, now there is a word. Scientific jargon comes much easier when you know some of the roots of words. Hemo means blood. Stasis means "to stand still" or stop. So when you put these two roots together, hemostasis is the process in which the body stops bleeding.

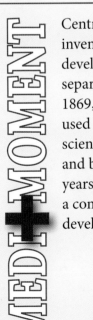

MED+MOMENT

Centrifuges came from an 1850 invention of a practical machine developed by Antonin Prandtl to separate cream from cows' milk. In 1869, scientist Friedrich Miescher used this device in a lab. Other scientists quickly saw the potential and began using it as well. Within 10 years of Miescher using the machine, a commercial centrifuge was developed by Gustaf de Laval.

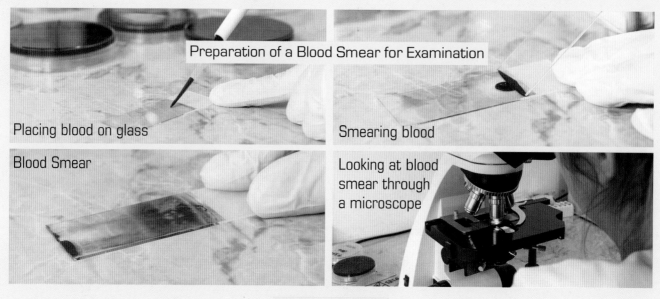

Preparation of a Blood Smear for Examination

Placing blood on glass

Smearing blood

Blood Smear

Looking at blood smear through a microscope

The Bottom Layer

Finally, the last layer is where the erythrocytes or red blood cells (RBC) reside. They are the heaviest components of blood. RBCs have a much higher concentration in the blood than white blood cells (WBC). For every 600 RBCs, there is 1 WBC! Red blood cells are biconcave in shape. They contain hemoglobin, an iron that carries the oxygen to our tissues and organs that need it for survival.

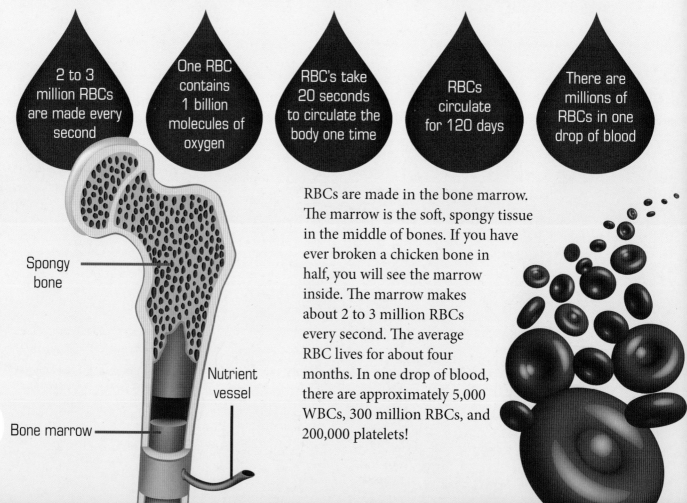

2 to 3 million RBCs are made every second

One RBC contains 1 billion molecules of oxygen

RBC's take 20 seconds to circulate the body one time

RBCs circulate for 120 days

There are millions of RBCs in one drop of blood

Spongy bone

Nutrient vessel

Bone marrow

RBCs are made in the bone marrow. The marrow is the soft, spongy tissue in the middle of bones. If you have ever broken a chicken bone in half, you will see the marrow inside. The marrow makes about 2 to 3 million RBCs every second. The average RBC lives for about four months. In one drop of blood, there are approximately 5,000 WBCs, 300 million RBCs, and 200,000 platelets!

Seeing Red

What is the color of your blood? That's an obvious question, right? Not so fast. There are many misconceptions that seem to continue to "circulate" in regard to this question. Most people, kids and adults alike, will say it is blue when it does not have much oxygen and when it hits the air or is rich with oxygen the color is red. Sound familiar? Many people believe this. After all, when you look at most books on the body, deoxygenated blood (blood with lower content of oxygen) in the illustrations is depicted blue. Blood rich in oxygen is depicted red. This is for illustration purposes only. Okay, how about this . . . if your skin is fair in color, why do the veins appear blue? All great observations! The actual lining of the blood vessels filters out certain light waves, and the color appears blue. Deoxygenated blood is actually a dark maroon color. It is never blue. The substance hemoglobin is an iron contained in RBCs that carries oxygen and gives our blood the familiar color red. Depending on the region of the country you live, you may be familiar to this process of oxygen reacting with a metal. The iron in a car can combine with oxygen in the air and form iron oxide. This causes the car to rust in areas. The mixture of iron and oxygen causes this familiar red color.

Hematopoiesis

Now that we have established the "recipe" for blood, how does our body "cook" up this wonderful thick substance? The process of making blood in our body is called hematopoiesis. Let's break that word down. Hemato comes from the Greek language meaning "blood." Poiesis has its origin in the Greek which means "the act of making or producing" something. Hematopoiesis is the formation of blood. When you were growing in your mother's womb, your blood was made in your spleen and liver. By the time you were born, your bone marrow in your long bones, such as your femur and tibia, had taken over the job of blood manufacturing. Blood cells are formed in the bones of the pelvis, skull, vertebrae (bones of the spine), and sternum (the breast bone) in adults.

Not all animals have red blood. There are creatures that do have blue blood. Can you think of any? Here is a hint. Animals that have blue blood have copper instead of iron in their blood.

The animals that have blue blood are horseshoe crabs, mollusks (snails, octopus, and squid), crustaceans (crabs, shrimp, and crayfish) and arachnids (spiders, scorpions, and tarantulas).

Hematopoiesis
blood cells are formed:

● Pelvis and Vertebra
● Sternum
● Ribs
● Lymph nodes
● Femur

29

All the cells in the blood originate from one common cell called a stem cell. The stem cells in the marrow have the ability to be any of the types of cells in the blood. All the cells in the blood begins as a stem cell. Starting at the stem cell, the cell divides into more and more specialized cells.

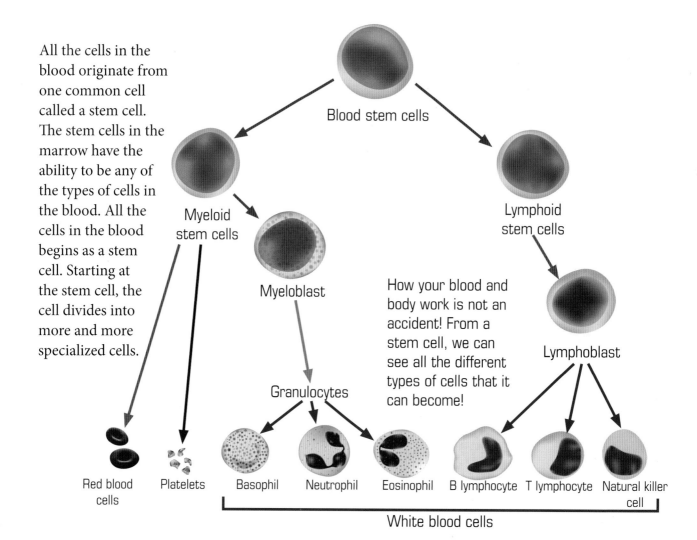

Blood stem cells

Myeloid stem cells

Lymphoid stem cells

Myeloblast

Lymphoblast

How your blood and body work is not an accident! From a stem cell, we can see all the different types of cells that it can become!

Granulocytes

Red blood cells

Platelets

Basophil

Neutrophil

Eosinophil

B lymphocyte

T lymphocyte

Natural killer cell

White blood cells

Bad Blood

One of the most common blood problems is anemia. Anemia occurs when you do not have enough red blood cells or the cells do not function properly. If you remember, red blood cells contain hemoglobin. This hemoglobin is important for the transport of oxygen throughout the body. People who suffer from anemia may experience tiredness, shortness of breath, dizziness, and pale skin. Anemia can be caused by things such as poor diet, intestine problems, and many diseases.

There are many types of anemia. Sickle cell anemia is one type of anemia. You cannot "catch" sickle cell anemia like a cold. It is a genetic disease that runs in families. Normally, a red blood cell has a nice flexible, smooth, and round contour. This allows the cells to glide through our vessels. In a person who suffers from sickle cell anemia, the red blood cell is rigid and sticky, and shaped like crescent moons. During a sickle cell crisis, a person will experience extreme pain. The sickled cells clump together. The cells will stick to the very walls of the blood vessels. These clumped cells block blood flow and cause damage to their organs like the brain, heart, bones, kidneys, and spleen to name a few.

Sickle cell is a disease that can be passed on in families whose origins began in Africa, India, and the Middle East. Interestingly, the disease is found more often on the continents where

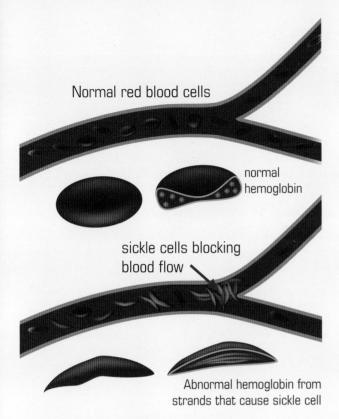

Normal red blood cells

normal hemoglobin

sickle cells blocking blood flow

Abnormal hemoglobin from strands that cause sickle cell

Abnormal, sickled, red blood cells (sickle cells)

the disease malaria is found. Malaria is a deadly disease transmitted by mosquitos. The malaria parasite, a small microscopic organism, is transmitted by mosquitos when they bite. Normally, this transmitted parasite will take residence in red blood cells. This parasite does not like sickle cells. In areas of the world where malaria is a problem, people born with sickle-cell anemia have an advantage in surviving malaria outbreaks. Two famous people who had or do have sickle cell anemia are Tiki Barber (a former NFL running back who played for the New York Giants) and Miles Davis (legendary jazz musician).

Put a Plug in It

Our blood tends to flow freely. When you skin your knee, this precious fluid leaks out. Have you ever stopped to wonder how your body stops the bleeding? This process is called hemostasis. It is the way the body stops you from bleeding. Let's take a look at this from the inside. Pretend you are a platelet floating along in the blood stream. Suddenly, as you approach the area of the knee, a small opening occurs in the blood vessels closest to the skin. The ragged edges expose collagen fibers that are connective tissue, usually confined within the vessel walls.

1. Spasms and Narrows: This damaged tissue of the blood vessel alerts the body to spring into action. Instantly, the blood vessel you are traveling in becomes narrowed. This is called vascular spasm. The body's response to narrowing the vessels in that area decreases the blood flowing out.

2. Plug the Hole: You move closer to the opening. Once you arrive at the opening, you stick to the edges of the open wound. Other friendly platelets join in, and you all stick together to plug up the opening. You all are held together by fibrin strands. You stick to the wound edges and wait for reinforcements. You release a protein called tissue factor (thromboplastin). Tissue factor is your mayday, a call for help to enlist help from prothrombin. The last stage occurs when the blood begins to clot.

3. Clotting Cascade: Prothrombin springs into action. Prothrombin is a special protein that is made in the liver. It circulates in the blood. It is not active but is ready to go to work when it is called into action by tissue factor. Prothrombin is activated and becomes thrombin. Red blood cells and white blood cells join the party. They stick close by you and your platelet friends. A cascade of events is triggered at this time. A cascade is like a stream or sequence of events occurring one after the other. Many other supporting factors spring into action in this miraculous cascade.

The blood in the area becomes gel-like, and a clot is formed. The hole is plugged up. Healing begins. The clot hardens and becomes a scab. New cells begin to grow and repair the wound area. Last, once the healing is complete, an enzyme is released to dissolve the clot.

Presto! The scab falls off, and you are healed! This is why you should not pick a scab. The scab is aiding in the healing process. The wound is not healed yet. If you pick the scab, you will begin to bleed a bit again.

In summary, the process of hemostasis occurs in three stages. First, the vessel spasms and narrows to slow down bleeding. Second, the platelets form a plug. Third, the blood-clotting cascade occurs. Crazy, right? The complexity of your body is amazing… even at levels you cannot see. The blood-clotting process truly demonstrates the genius of our great God.

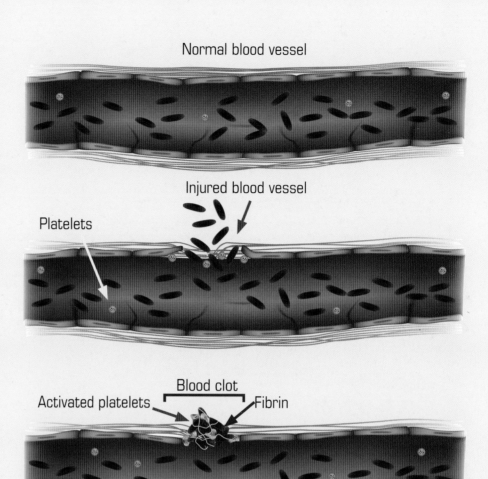

Normal blood vessel

Injured blood vessel

Platelets

Blood clot

Activated platelets — Fibrin

How your blood and body work is not an accident! From a stem cell, we can see all the different types of cells that it can become!

Hemophilia: The Royal Disease

Sometimes things can go wrong in the body. The clotting system can be overactive and form clots blocking blood flow to areas of the body. Sometimes the clotting system doesn't clot when an injury occurs in the case of a rare genetic condition called hemophilia. It is a disease that runs in families and is not contagious. People who suffer from hemophilia are lacking one of the items in the blood-clotting cascade that makes them unable to form a clot. Hemophilia has no cure. We do have ways to help a hemophilic in the face of an emergency. The item or factor that they are missing can be given to them intravenously (via a vein) and can be life-saving.

Prince Leopold

Hemophilia affects boys more than girls. Hemophilia has not always been understood. It has a debilitating history. In 19th-century Europe, during the rule of Great Britain's Queen Victoria (1819–1901), a disease was playing havoc with the royal family. The royal family felt it was important to keep their blood lines "pure." The royal family would marry other family members, like first cousins, so as not to taint the royal line with other blood. Due to this intermarrying of family members, diseases that could be passed on to other family members were more common and severe.

Prince Leopold, the Duke of Albany, was Queen Victoria's eighth child. He was considered to be "very delicate." He suffered many life-threatening bleeding episodes. Because of his fragile nature, he was constantly monitored by the royal staff. Unfortunately, Prince Leopold died when he was 31 years old due to a minor injury.

Darwin's Corner

Creationists and evolutionists are at odds with each other in regard to life's origins. Evolutionists believe that human life evolved from the simplest life forms to the complexity we see in our bodies today. In Genesis 1 it states God created plants and animals to reproduce according to their kinds. A turnip can not produce a grape. A single-celled microscopic organism does not produce a human.

Evolutionists have used the disease sickle cell anemia as one of their defenses for evolution. The illness of malaria is devastating. It kills approximately 2 million people a year. People who suffer from sickle cell anemia are "protected" from the malaria parasite transmitted by mosquitoes. Their blood cells are fragile and "sickle," crushing the parasite. Evolutionists defend that people who have this one amino acid mutation in their hemoglobin that causes the sickling are at an evolutional advantage over others. They cannot contract malaria, and therefore sickle cell is beneficial. I don't believe any of us would request this "minor" substitution in one of our amino acids to give us immunity from malaria. Sickle cell anemia is a extremely painful genetic disorder that causes life long problems. To sum it up, sickle cell anemia is caused due to a mutation that is not favorable for the recipient and not a defense for evolution.

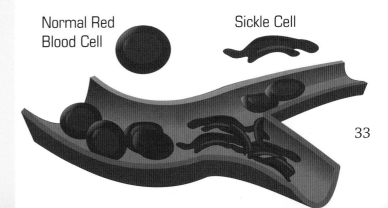

Normal Red Blood Cell

Sickle Cell

You're Not My Type

Blood has always had an air of mystery about it. The earliest accounts of blood transfusion met with disastrous results. One of the earliest recorded transfusions was performed by Jean-Baptiste Denis (physician to Louis XIV of France) in 1667. His patient was a man who was considered "mad." The man would wander through the streets of Paris unclothed, was abusive to his wife, and set houses on fire during his fits. Dr. Denis thought if perhaps he trans-fused blood from a gentle lamb into the man that he would become calm. After a few transfusions, the man became very ill. He no longer had the energy to beat his wife or to set things ablaze. In the minds of everyone, this treatment was successful! After his recovery, the man returned to his old ways. His distressed wife begged Dr. Denis to redo his treatments. Dr. Denis refused. Sadly, the woman, feeling she could take no more, poisoned her husband. Due to this act, blood transfusions were banned in France and Great Britain, and by the pope.

The buzz about the ability to transfuse blood from one person to another began to resurface in the early 1820s. James Blundell, in 1828, is credited for introducing the concept of blood transfusions as a potentially life-saving procedure. He was an obste-trician, a doctor who cares for pregnant women, at Guy's Hospital in London. A woman who had just delivered her baby began to bleed profusely. He transfused her with blood donated from her husband. It was a success. Unfortunately, for the next 70 years, the success of transfusion medicine was unpredictable. Some people survived after a transfusion, but many people would die shortly after a transfusion.

A lancet used to draw blood.

Solving the Mystery

Austrian born Karl Landsteiner was able to put the pieces together for the puzzling problems of blood transfusion. He identified that although blood from all people looked alike, that there were differences in blood types. He identified four major blood types: A, B, AB, and O. The differences lay in the presence or absence in A or B antigens. Antigens are substances found on cells. It can activate the immune system to produce antibodies against foreign invaders. Antibodies are a distress call that signals the body to send white blood cells to defend and protect the body from foreign invasion. When blood from a person is given to a person with a different blood type, then the body's immune system springs to action. The blood will clump and causes a reaction that can be deadly.

Group O can donate red blood cells to anybody. It's the universal donor.

Group A can donate red blood cells to A's and AB's

Group B can donate red blood cells to B's and AB's

Group AB can donate to other AB's, but can receive from all others.

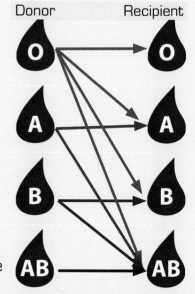

Donor   Recipient

People with blood type AB are called "universal" receivers. They can receive blood from any blood type. AB contains both A and B antigens but has no antibodies. A person with blood type O is called a "universal" donor. O contains no antigens but contains both anti-A and anti-B antibodies.

During World War II, plasma, one of the components of blood, was found to be vitally useful in treating wounded soldiers. It was easier to transport. The red blood cells were removed so there was no need to match blood types of the donor with the recipient. Dr. Charles Drew, developed these techniques. He worked with the American Red Cross to establish blood banks, or bloodmobiles, which were trucks serving as donation centers. In addition to the A and B antigens, there is a third antigen called the Rh (Rhesus) factor. When present it is marked with a plus (+), when not present it is negative (−). People with Rh negative blood can only receive blood from other Rh negative donors. People with Rh positive can receive Rh negative or Rh positive blood.

Your blood type was determined and passed onto you based on the genetic makeup of your parents.

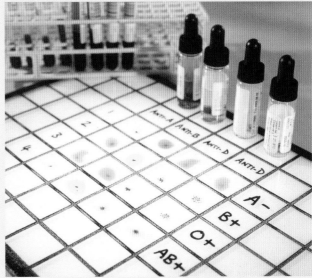

Blood typing tests (pictured) can occur before transfusions or during pregnancies. Results are determined though the reactions shown. Type A blood has type A antigens on its blood cells and anti-B antibodies in its serum. Type B blood is the reverse. Mixing type A blood with anti-A antibodies leads to a clumping reaction, which is seen as dense red dots. AB blood has both A and B antigens on its cells, but no antibodies. Type O blood has no antigens and both antibodies. Anti-D is an antibody used to test for Rhesus antigens (which point to some prenatal diseases), and it reacts with Rhesus positive blood.

Blood Type Percentages by Ethnicity

	Caucasians	African American	Hispanic	Asian
O+	37%	47%	53%	39%
O−	8%	4%	4%	1%
A+	33%	24%	29%	27%
A−	7%	2%	2%	0.5%
B+	9%	18%	9%	25%
B−	2%	1%	1%	0.4%
AB+	3%	4%	2%	7%
AB−	1%	0.3%	0.2%	0.1%

3 Highways of Blood

Inside your body is a small universe. The blood vessels that travel to every nook and cranny in your body are impressive. If you were to take all the vessels and line them up end to end, they would expand a distance of 60,000 miles!

As you read this section, it may be helpful to have a picture of the heart nearby. Starting on the left side of the heart, the oxygenated blood is pumped into the largest artery of the body called the aorta. The aorta has two large branches — the ascending goes upward, and the descending goes downward. You may have observed your descending aorta pulsating. If you lie on your back and watch your stomach, you may see it slightly bouncing up and down at the same rate as your heart beats. This is your abdominal aorta artery.

Arteries in your body carry blood that is rich in oxygen. The blood in these vessels is bright red. The size of the arteries traveling through your body, run from largest to the smallest. The flow runs from the arteries to the arterioles, and then to the smallest, which are called capillaries. The aorta measures about an inch in diameter. The capillaries are tiny. They are about 1/3000th of an inch in diameter. That is about a tenth the diameter of a human hair! The capillaries are so small that blood cells have to line up in single file to pass. Sometimes the cells have to bend their shapes even to pass through the small orifice (opening). (Remember when we talked about sickle cell anemia earlier? This is why sickle cell anemia is so painful. The sickled cells are not flexible and have jagged edges. They tear the capillary walls. This blocks blood flow. This causes a very painful crisis.) Capillaries are extremely helpful. The blood flow slows down to pass. Your organs and cells are able to extract what they need from the blood, from oxygen to nutrients, and deposits waste products.

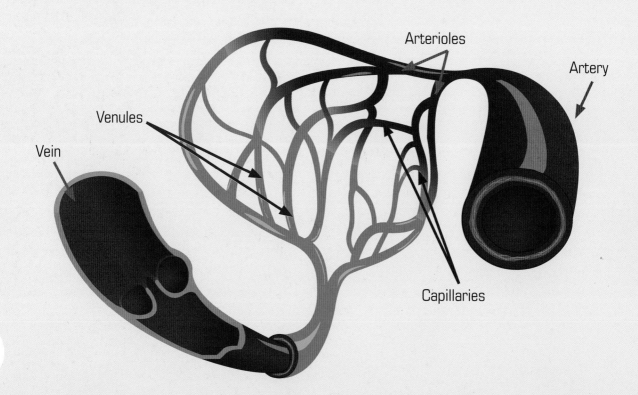

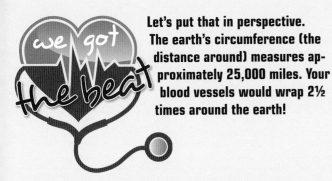

we got the beat

Let's put that in perspective. The earth's circumference (the distance around) measures approximately 25,000 miles. Your blood vessels would wrap 2½ times around the earth!

Once the blood clears the arterial system (arteries, arterioles, and capillaries), it needs to begin its journey back to the heart. The red blood cells need to be reloaded with oxygen. Your organs and cells throws out the "garbage" from all of its hard work. One of the garbage items that is thrown out is carbon dioxide. The red blood cells pick this up. They transport the garbage (carbon dioxide) to the lungs. This is where you breathe in oxygen and exhale carbon dioxide. The blood enters the venous system once it leaves the arterial system.

The venous system vessels run from the small vessels to the large. The veins carry deoxygenated blood. The blood is maroon in color. The capillaries flow and connect to a network of vessels called the capillary network, which connect to the veins. The smallest veins are called venules. The venules expand to larger vessels called veins. The veins are the the ones that appear blue under your skin. The larger veins run to the right side of the heart.

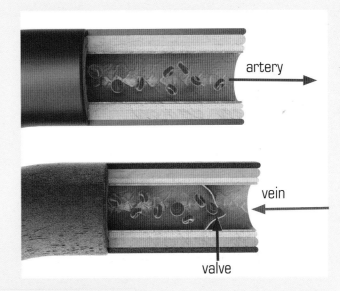

artery

vein

valve

Comparison of arteries to veins chart

Comparisons	Arteries	Veins
Oxygen content	Carries oxygenated blood	Carries deoxygenated blood
Direction of blood flow	Away from the heart	Toward the heart
Construction of the vessel	Thick and rubber-band like, which helps handle higher pressure and blood flow. Vessels are more rigid.	Thinner; vessels are easily compressible
Location	Can be deeper inside the body	Superficial in the body; lie closer to surface of the skin
Valves	Do not have valves	Have valves inside preventing the blood from flowing backward. Blood in veins works against gravity to get the blood back to the heart.

Blood helps to keep us alive. There are creatures that not only have their own blood supply, but they feast on the blood of others. I know on many summer nights I have provided a tasty snack for hematophagic mosquitos. Hematophagy is the scientific name for the practice of animals feeding on blood. Hemato means blood; phagy means to eat or feed.

**Below you will find a list, of a few animals that feed on blood.
Can you think of others?**

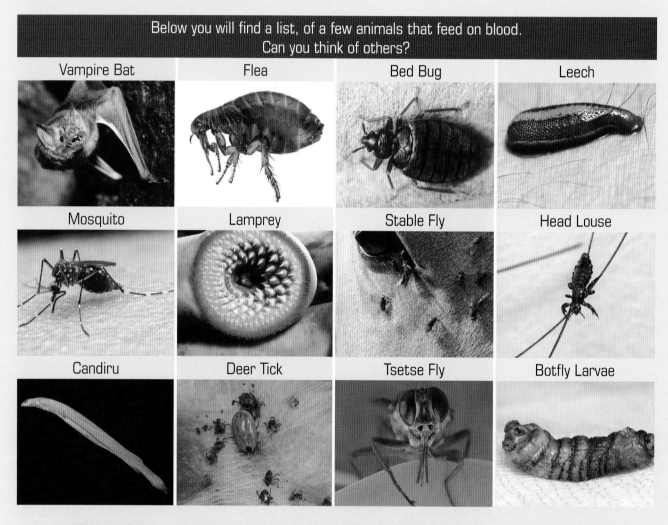

Vampire Bat   Flea   Bed Bug   Leech

Mosquito   Lamprey   Stable Fly   Head Louse

Candiru   Deer Tick   Tsetse Fly   Botfly Larvae

Mosquitos do have blood in their bodies. Whack! Have you ever caught a mosquito in the act of feeding on you? It is "kinda" messy after you forcefully "convince" the mosquito to stop their snacking. The blood you see does not belong to her! Mosquitos have clear blood! They do not have any metals in their blood to give it the red color.

we got the beat

I know everyone has their own favorite bloodsuckers, right? Here are three of my favorites:

Ticks

Mosquitoes

There are more than 800 species in the tick family — it makes for quite a crowded family reunion. Some ticks are hard bodied. Some ticks are soft bodied. They inject a chemical that keeps their victim's blood from clotting. This allows them to get their "money's worth" when they go out to dinner. Their preferred dining location is biting around the head, neck, and ears of their blood "donors." Ticks need blood to grow and live. They normally reside in warmer climates that are humid, with wooded areas.

There are many tick-borne illnesses. Ticks transmit illness through their saliva. Some tick-borne illnesses are Rickettsia, Colorado tick fever, Rocky Mountain spotted fever, relapsing fever, and of course, Lyme disease, to name a few. Look out for the tick's close cousin, *Ixodes Scapularis*. He is known as the deer tick and is a known to be a carrier of Lyme disease.

Ticks track down mammals, like us, by sensing carbon dioxide. When we exhale carbon dioxide, the dinner bell rings for the tick and dinner is served. They utilize their mouth parts to clasp on and plunge their barb-like needle into the skin. They attach and commence dining. Ticks suck in the blood and dine for a few days until they become engorged and fall off.

Next up is the mosquito. Their name originates from the Spanish word *musketas,* which means little flies. A mosquito's wings flap 300 to 400 times each second. You may have encountered her annoying buzzing around your ears during a camping trip. The ladies of the mosquito family are the only ones who dine on blood. They love blood most when it is close to the time of egg laying. She only has a life span of about 14 days so she will probably have to eat and run.

The males of the family don't find blood palatable. They prefer the sweet taste of nectar from plants and flowers. Mosquitos can also be disease carriers. They can transmit diseases through their salvia, like yellow fever, West Nile, and malaria.

Mosquitos find some people's blood more "tasty" than others. Mosquitos prefer to feed more on people with type O blood, heavy breathers (lots of carbon dioxide attracts them), sweaty people, and women who are pregnant. A natural way to keep these insects away is to use lavender on your skin or eat lots of garlic. When you eat garlic, you sweat it, and mosquitos hate the smell. As a matter of fact, it may keep people away also.

Last, but not least, is the leech. They have a great family history that is as long as recorded time. Leeches are a type of worm. However, leeches are hermaphrodites, which means they are both male and female all rolled up in one.

Leeches, in early times, were used for bloodletting. They were considered easier to use than a lancet in Middle Ages to restore the "humors" back in order. They have suckers on both ends of their bodies that attach to the victim. They can grow five times their size with a good, filling meal. They do not let go until they have completed their meal.

Leeches are no longer used for bloodletting today, but they are used for "hirudotherapy." Hirudo is a type of leech. The Hirudo medicinalis leech is used in medicine. It has three jaws that cut like sharp razors into the skin. Once the skin is cut

by the leech, it injects several substances. One substance is called hirudin. (This is where it gets its name.) This substance keeps the blood from clotting. Hirudin blocks fibrin from forming in a blood clot. Like the mosquito and tick, they inject an anesthetic, a substance that prohibits pain, into the wound. After all, they don't want their dining pleasure interrupted.

So the question remains — how on earth are they used in medicine? I am glad you asked. In the United States, leeches are considered a "medical device." Leeches are utilized after surgery in some cases for skin that has been reattached.

One of the problems with reattachment of skin from reconstructive surgery is that blood clots can form in the natural healing process and cause the area to die due to lack of blood supply. The leeches' talents are called into action. During a

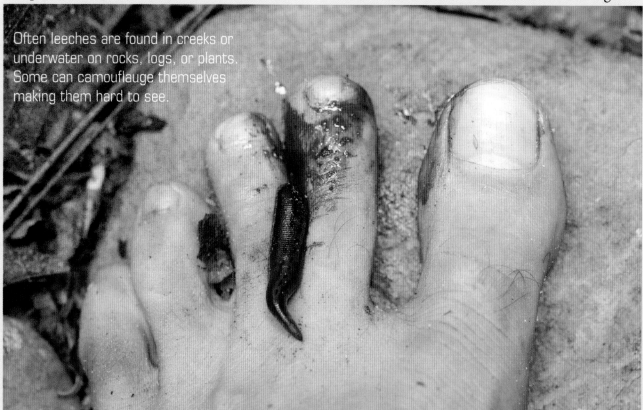

Often leeches are found in creeks or underwater on rocks, logs, or plants. Some can camouflauge themselves making them hard to see.

There are over 700 species of leeches in the world, though one type is is only used medically. They are used in areas related to arthritis, disorders of the blood, varicose veins, and in some plastic surgery procedures.

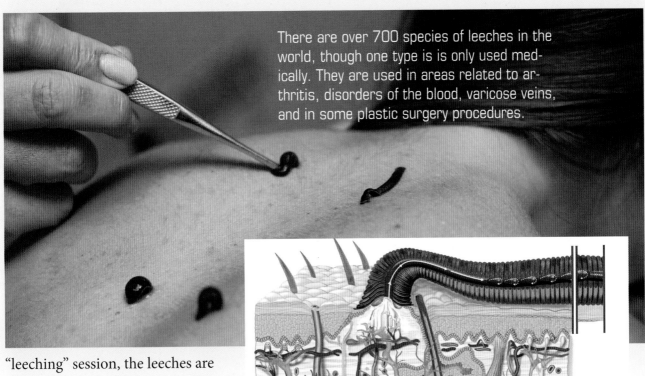

"leeching" session, the leeches are allowed to attach in the surgical area. They release into the skin the blood-thinning and clot-preventing chemicals. It gladly ingests the extra blood that accumulates in the area. The benefit is that it improves the blood circulation by breaking up the problematic clots, and this promotes healing.

Bloodsucking at its best. A leech attaching to the skin releases two chemicals into the local vessels that thins the blood and keeps it from clotting. This helps the leech enjoy a tasty meal longer.

Word Wise!

LEECHES used to be the common name given to people in Europe and North Americas who worked as healers or physicians centuries ago, and "to leech" meant to heal or cure someone. The use of leeches can be traced back to ancient India and Greece, Now, the term "leech" is used as to describe clinging to someone constantly or taking needed resources like money away from you.

We now arrive at the "heart" of the matter. The blood and the vessels in our bodies could not work effectively if it weren't for our beating hearts. It weighs only about 11 ounces. (A pound is 16 ounces.) The largest heart known is that of the blue whale. It tips the scale at 1,500 pounds, which is the size of a small car. The aorta of the blue whale is large enough for an adult to crawl through. The average heart beats about 100,000 times a day. In an adult, the heart pumps 2,000 gallons in a day. Whew! I am exhausted just thinking about it.

We have what is called a closed circulatory system. A closed circulatory system means that blood travels only within the blood vessels and the heart. It does not ooze into our body cavities. An open circulatory system is seen in many insects, mollusks, and crustaceans. Blood in these animals is pumped by the heart into the body cavity where the organs are bathed. It is crazy, but it has been shown that if a cockroach's head is cut off, after the blood clots up the opening, that it can live up to one month! It ultimately dies due to starvation.

The Outside of the Heart

Let's take a look at the anatomy of the heart from the outside in. The heart lies in the chest underneath your sternum (breast bone). Your heart is about the size of your fist. It is encased in a double-layered sac called the pericardial sac. Peri means around. Cardi means heart. The sac's purpose is to cut down the friction generated by your constantly beating heart. A small amount of fluid exists between the layers of the sac that allows the membranes to slide freely without friction.

Have you ever had an opportunity to look at a real heart from a chicken or cow? Some people like to eat livestock hearts. It is a muscle that some find very tasty. Looking at the surface, you will notice blood vessels that travel on the outside of the heart. All the gallons of blood that run through the inside of the heart are for use by the whole body. The vessels outside of the heart are for the personal circulatory system of the heart. These are called the coronary arteries and veins. A heart attack (or medically speaking, a myocardial infarction) is the result of one or more of the coronary arteries becoming blocked. Once

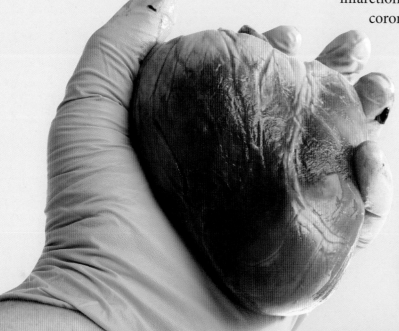

Your heart is about the size of your fist. It beats from 4-5 weeks of conception in your mother's womb until the day you take your last breath. It is without a doubt the strongest muscle in your body.

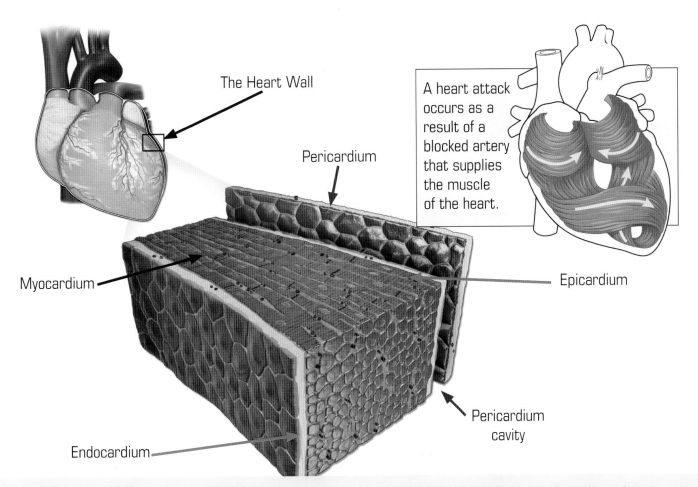

The Heart Wall

Pericardium

A heart attack occurs as a result of a blocked artery that supplies the muscle of the heart.

Myocardium

Epicardium

Endocardium

Pericardium cavity

the artery is blocked, the tissue lying downstream from the block does not receive blood. If it doesn't receive blood, it doesn't receive oxygen and nutrients. It begins to die.

The actual muscle of the heart is composed of three layers. The outer part of the muscle, lying under the pericardial sac, is called the epicardium. The epicardium literally means the outer part of the heart. The middle layer is called the myocardium. Myo means muscle. The most inner layer is called the endocardium (inside the heart).

I bet you will be amazed at how much you already know. I will give you three heart diseases. Can you tell me where each of them occur? Oh, yes, here is one more hint before you take a whack at it — any word that ends with "itis" means that something is inflamed or infected.

Are you ready? What do the words endocarditis, myocarditis, and pericarditis mean?

Endocarditis	An infection of the inner lining of the heart.
Myocarditis	is an infection of the myocardium, the middle layer of the heart wall. Myocarditis can affect both the heart's muscle cells and the heart's electrical system, leading to reduction in the heart's pumping function and to irregular heart rhythms.
Pericarditis	is swelling, irritation, or infection of the pericardium, the thin, sac-like membrane surrounding your heart.

43

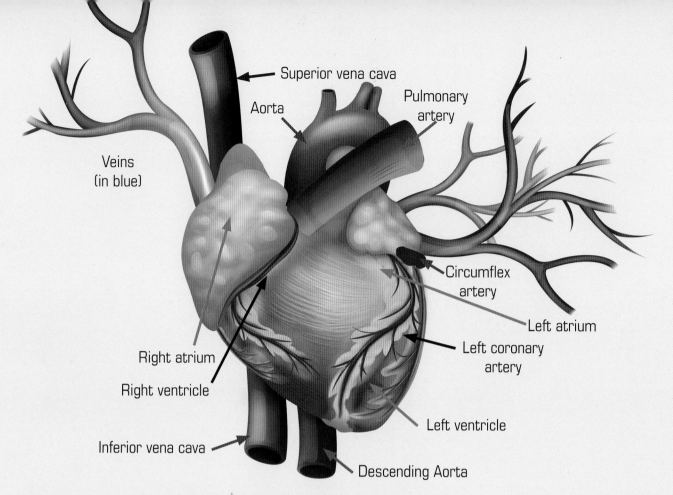

Superior vena cava

Aorta

Pulmonary artery

Veins (in blue)

Circumflex artery

Left atrium

Left coronary artery

Right atrium

Right ventricle

Left ventricle

Inferior vena cava

Descending Aorta

The Inside of the Heart: Going with the Flow

Allright, budding cardiologists, now we will take a look at the four chambers, or rooms, of the heart. There are two upper rooms and two lower rooms. The upper rooms are called atrium. Atrium means entrance in Latin. The lower rooms are called ventricles. Ventricles are derived from the Latin word meaning "little belly." The heart is similar to two pumps. The right side pumps the blood to the lungs. The left side pumps the blood to the entire body. Follow the numbers labeled on the following heart diagram on page 45 as you read the following descriptions.

Numbers 1–2: Deoxygenated blood (blood lower in oxygen concentration) enters the right side of the heart through the right atrium via two great veins. The superior vena cava brings blood from the upper part of the body. The inferior vena cava brings blood from the lower part of the body. The

chambers and great vessels have "doors" separating them from the next room. These "doors" are called valves. The valves in the chambers are connected by cords to the floor of the heart. This ensures that the valves swing open in one direction and blood travels in one direction, forward. The cords are called the chordae tendineae. There is an old expression, "You're tugging on my heart strings," that may have originated from these cardiac strings. (It means to cause someone to feel more emotional.)

Numbers 3–4–5: From the right atrium, blood travels through the door of the tricuspid valve into the right ventricle. Blood is then pushed into the pulmonary artery past the pulmonary semilunar valves to be oxygenated in the lungs.

Numbers 6–7–8: Once oxygenated, it is returned to the left atrium of the heart via the pulmonary veins, by being pushed through the mitral valve (bicuspid valve) into the left ventricle.

Numbers 9–10: Finally, with great force, the blood is ejected out into the aorta artery past the aortic semilunar valve to the rest of the body. It takes approximately a minute when you are at rest for the blood to circumnavigate the full trip of the

body. The time can be less, depending on the heart rate and size of the heart.

Did you notice any "errors" in that last paragraph? Take another look. You may have been savvy to pick up on something about the pulmonary artery and pulmonary vein. Normally, arteries carry oxygenated blood and veins carry deoxygenated blood. This is the only contradiction in the body. The pulmonary artery and vein carry the opposite. They are named this way because of how they are formed in fetal development.

Flow of the Blood through the Heart: Follow the numbered arrows through the heart as the blood flows from the right side of the heart, through the lungs to the left side of the heart. The numbers 1 through 10 depicts the sequence. Blue depicts deoxygenated blood. Red depicts oxygenated blood.

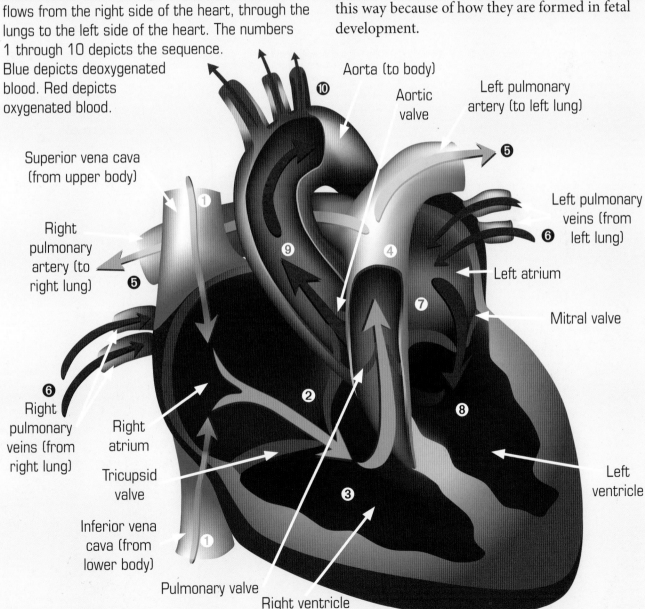

45

The Beat Goes On

"Lub-dub. Lub-dub. Lub-dub" is the characteristic sound heard when you listen to someone's heart. Lub is the first sound heard, dub is the second sound. The sounds that you hear when listening to a heart are actually the doors (valves) slamming shut in the heart. The first sound, lub, is the closure of the tricuspid and mitral valves between the atria and ventricles. The second sound, dub, is heard at the closure of the pulmonary semilunar valves as the blood is pushed into the lungs. The aortic valve also closes as blood is ejected to the rest of the body.

The heart has its own electrical circuitry that runs in its muscular walls. The beat of the heart is controlled by special cardiac muscle cells that deliver an electrical charge that causes the heart to beat. There are two special areas in the right atrium that trigger the beat of the heart. The sinoatrial (SA) node located on the top of the right atrium is the pacemaker. It controls the pace, or how fast the heart beats. It is like the pace car at a motor car race that goes ahead of the other cars to set the rate.

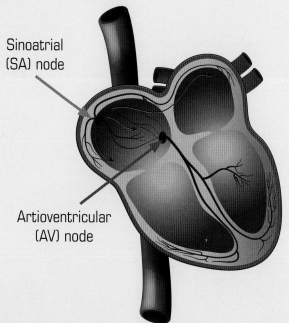

Sinoatrial
(SA) node

Artioventricular
(AV) node

The charge travels from the SA node down to the lower portion of the right atrium to the second area called the atrioventricular (AV) node. From here, the electrical impulse travels down the middle (intraventricular septum) between the right and left ventricles and travels around the outside walls of the heart. The heart has its own internal regulatory system. The heart will beat and continue to have some electrical activity for a couple of minutes after it is removed. (This is not recommended.)

Your heart is the only muscle in your body that does not get tired. The "rest" it takes is very short. Systole is the contraction phase of the heart when blood is pushed forward. Diastole is the only time the heart takes a small pause to "rest." What really happens during diastole is that the heart pauses briefly to allow the blood to refill the heart.

The heart also has a control system that can override the internal system. A nerve control system in the brain stem in the medulla oblongata is an essential partner in regulating the heart. Sometimes your heart needs to speed up or slow down. This area in the brain stem secretes chemicals that will speed up or slow down the heart, depending on the body's demands. For example, if you decided to go to Spain and participate in the event called the "Running of the Bulls," this will come in quite handy. You step out on the street with hundreds of your closest friends. The bulls are let loose down the streets. You begin to run for your life. Your heart will need to speed up to keep up with the oxygen demand of your body. Your legs start to pump. Your heart rate speeds up. Presto! You are able to dive out of the way of a snorting angry bull!

The Electrocardiogram

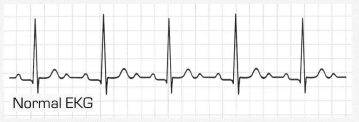

Normal EKG

Have you ever seen these kind of images? They are a tracing from an electrocardiogram (ECG or EKG) machine. The electrical activity of the heart is present all the time. We have this special machine that can record the electrical activity without cutting inside the body. It causes no pain. A series of electrodes in a special foamy adhesive tape is placed on various locations on the chest over the heart. The series of spikes and dips, like a rollercoaster, are documented. These waves record normal or abnormal activity of the heart.

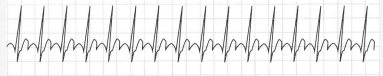

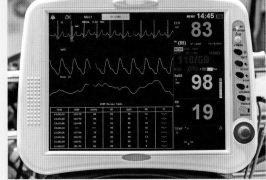

In some people, the heart beats too fast. This is called tachycardia. Tachy means fast.

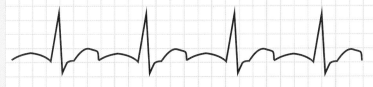

Sometimes the heart beats too slowly. This is called bradycardia. Brady means to slow.

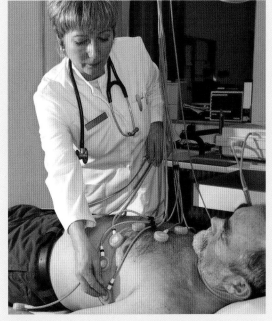

Sometimes the heart's electrical activity is irregular and inconsistent. This is a tracing called fibrillation. The muscle of the heart does not beat in a synchronized fashion. When this happens, the heart is unable to pump blood. This is dangerous.

All of these types of rhythms can be unhealthy for a person. These are called arrhythmias (irregular rates). God has given doctors, scientists, and technicians the reasoning ability to find solutions to some of these problems. A pacemaker can be a useful tool in controlling an irregular rhythm. It is a small electrical device surgically placed in someone's chest or abdomen under the skin to assist in controlling abnormal heart rates. It monitors the heart internally. If an irregular rhythm occurs, it sends a very low electrical pulse to prompt the heart to get back on track.

47

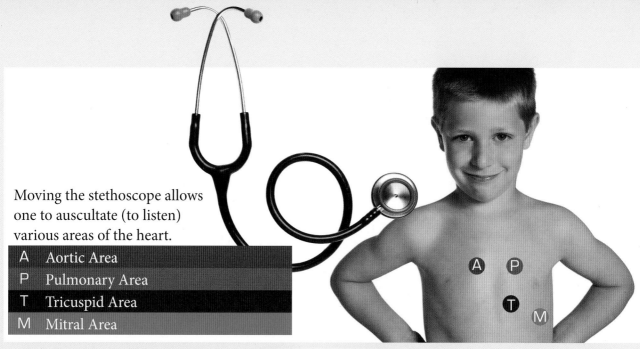

Moving the stethoscope allows one to auscultate (to listen) various areas of the heart.

A	Aortic Area
P	Pulmonary Area
T	Tricuspid Area
M	Mitral Area

Listen to My Heart

It is truly incredible what God will do in our lives when we turn our hearts to Him and listen. Listening is one of the most powerful tools we can develop in learning about our world and growing in our faith. Listening is a skill that doctors must develop in caring for their patients. It is essential to listen to someone as they explain their symptoms. It is also critical to listen to the sounds of the body. As a pediatrician, a children's doctor, I have seen that many of my smallest patients are unable to use words to explain what troubles them. When I listen to the hearts of my patients, I close my eyes and focus intently on the sounds. In the same way, I prefer to close my eyes and bow my head when I pray. It takes all the other distractions away. I am better at concentrating and listening.

During a visit to the doctor, you may have noticed that the doctor listened to your chest with a stethoscope. The stethoscope is a medical device that doctors, nurses, and other health professionals use to listen to the sounds of the body. You may have also noticed that the stethoscope was moved to various locations on your chest. Moving the stethoscope allows one to auscultate (to listen) various areas of the heart.

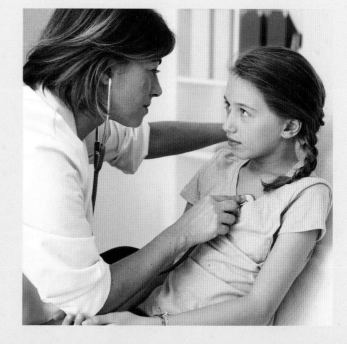

I AM wonderfully made

But in your hearts revere Christ as Lord. Always be prepared to give an answer to everyone who asks you to give the reason for the hope that you have. But do this with gentleness and respect (1 Peter 3:15).

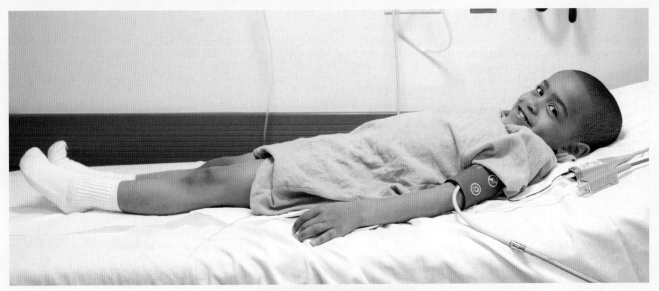

Feeling Under Pressure

As your heart beats, it forces the blood through the blood vessels at a certain pressure. Let's say you took a long balloon and filled it with water. You squeeze the water out the other end with a great force. The water would rush out under the pressure generated by the force of your hand. This is what happens in your blood vessels. The higher the pressure in your vessels, the harder your heart works.

We can measure this pressure with an instrument called a sphygmomanometer. Try saying that ten times fast! The cuff is placed around the arm, just above the bend in the elbow. The blood pressure cuff is inflated snug enough to stop the blood flow in the vessels for just a moment. Slowly the air is let out of the cuff. It slowly deflates. Listening with a stethoscope over the vessels in the fold of your arm, you will begin to hear the pulse and rush of the blood through the vessel. The cuff deflates. You will hear a beginning sound. The sound will persist for several beats until no sound is heard anymore. Watching the gauge, you will note when the first

sound and last sound is noted. The first reading is the systolic pressure. This is the highest pressure the heart generated at the peak of its contraction. The second reading is the diastolic pressure. This is the pressure during the relaxation of the ventricles.

A normal blood pressure for an adult is 120/80. The pressure in children varies, depending on the age of the child. Healthy newborn babies will have lower blood pressure. Typically, their blood pressure is about 64/41. Why do you think there would be such a difference in a baby's blood pressure compared to an adult?

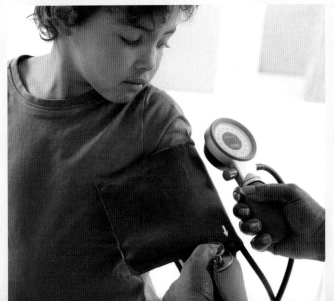

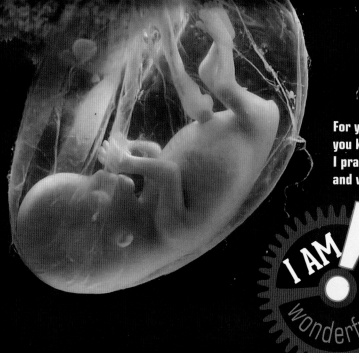

For you created my inmost being;
you knit me together in my mother's womb.
I praise you because I am fearfully
and wonderfully made;your works are wonderful,
I know that full well.
My frame was not hidden from you
when I was made in the secret place,
when I was woven together in the
depths of the earth.
Your eyes saw my unformed body;
all the days ordained for me were
written in your book
before one of them came to be.

– Psalm 139:13–16

I AM! wonderfully made

we got the beat

In the mother's womb, after the baby is conceived, by the fifth week, the heart of the baby starts beating and divides into chambers. Six weeks later blood is flowing inside the body. The heart rate is approximately 160 beats every minute.

Your heart began development as a simple tube with trunks on each end. It began to beat when you were in your mother's womb, at about 3–4 weeks. The circulatory system is the first major system to function. The heart tube grows longer and then bends back on itself as a loop. The folding of the heart tube only takes 6 days. A four-chambered heart is formed from this convoluted tube. The dividers between the chambers are called septa. They form from the grooves between the folds. The dividers fuse to make walls between the chambers. However, a small hole does remain between the top atrium to allow the blood to be taken directly from the right to the left side of the heart. It is called the foramen ovale. This allows the blood to bypass (go around) the lungs.

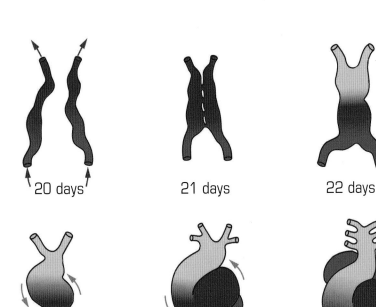

20 days

21 days

22 days

23 days

24 days

35 days

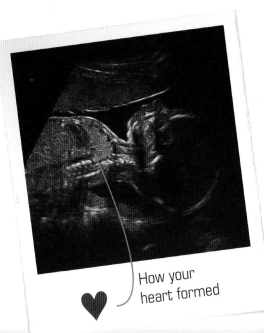

How your heart formed

Your heart begins as two tubes that fuse together, and it folds and molds itself into a two-system pump. The right side of the heart pumps blood to your lungs. The left side of the heart pumps the blood to the rest of the entire body.

FETAL HEART RATES

Starting at week 5 the fetal heart rate accelerates by 3.3 beats per minute (bpm) per day for the next month.

The fetal heart begins to beat at the same rate as the mother's, which is typically 80 to 85 beats per minute.

Week 5	starts at 80 and ends at 103 bpm
Week 6	starts at 103 and ends at 126 bpm
Week 8	starts at 126 and ends at 149 bpm
Week 9	the fetal heartbeat tends to beat within a range of 155 to 195 bpm

At this point, the fetal heart rate begins to decrease, and generally falls within the range of 120 to 160 bpm by week 12.

In the womb, the lungs receive blood for nourishment purposes only. The lungs do not provide oxygen for the baby. The blood circulation in a fetus, a baby in the womb, is different than the blood circulation in you and me. There are two major shunts (short cuts). The shunts are small passageways that bypass the lungs and liver. The liver and lungs are not fully developed while the fetus is in the womb. The placenta, the structure that connects the mother to the baby, does the work of these organs. The placenta provides all the oxygen and nourishment the baby needs from the mother. Babies do not "breathe" inside the womb. The environment that the baby lives in is filled with fluid.

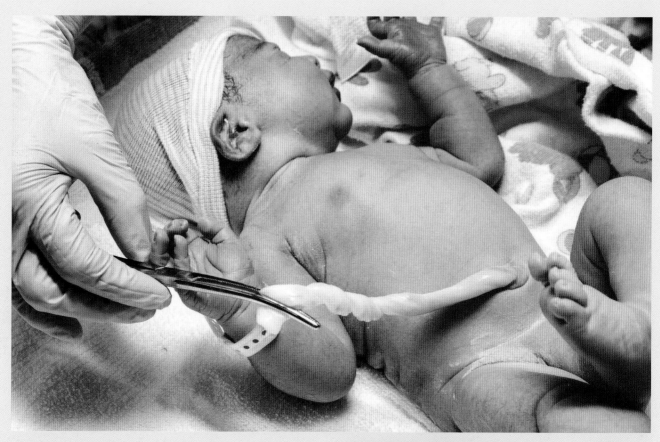

At birth, the baby's first cry starts the miraculous conversion of the fetal circulation to the baby breathing on its own. The umbilical cord, the tube that connects the mother to the baby by way of the placenta, is clamped off at birth.

Now the baby must do things on its own. What is left of your umbilical cord dries up and falls off. You don't need it any more. You are left with your wonderful belly button. Your first cry rushes oxygen into your lungs. This oxygen signals the shunts in your body to close down. They did a great job for you when you were in the womb. They are no longer needed now.

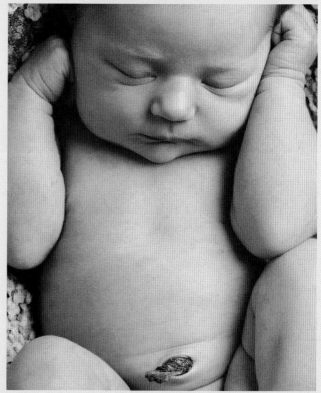

The picture below illustrates fetal circulation. The five vessels in the box below (formen ovale, umbilical vein, umbilical artery, ductus arteriosus, and ductus venosus) are vessels that close down at birth. They are no longer necessary after birth.

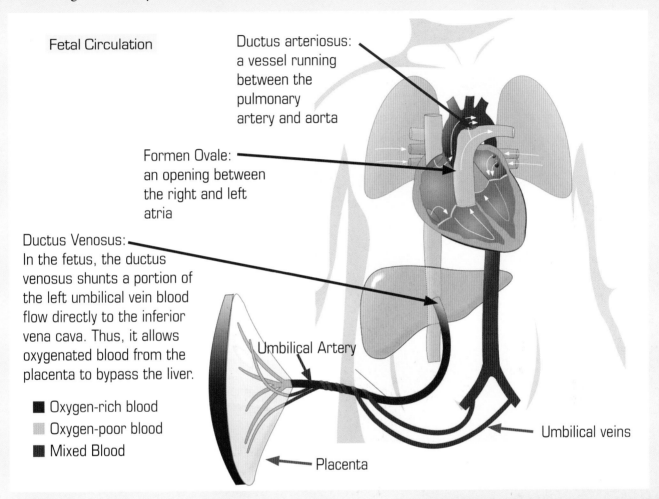

Fetal Circulation

Ductus arteriosus: a vessel running between the pulmonary artery and aorta

Formen Ovale: an opening between the right and left atria

Ductus Venosus: In the fetus, the ductus venosus shunts a portion of the left umbilical vein blood flow directly to the inferior vena cava. Thus, it allows oxygenated blood from the placenta to bypass the liver.

■ Oxygen-rich blood
■ Oxygen-poor blood
■ Mixed Blood

Umbilical Artery

Umbilical veins

Placenta

Some children are born with heart defects. At some point when the heart was developing, it did not form correctly. You may have heard of someone who was born with a "hole" in their heart. This is a defect or hole in the walls between the ventricle or atrium. Some of the blood does not go to the lungs and goes directly from the right side of the heart to the left side. There are many different types of defects. Millions of people have been born with a heart defect, which are among the most common birth defects. Some defects don't need to be treated. For those that do, thanks to medical advances and new types of surgeries, today most are able to have the defect repaired.

Heart Surgery Robots

Robots performing surgery? Sounds like the stuff from which science fiction movies are made. It truly is a reality!

Introducing the "da Vinci" surgical system. It is inspired from Leonardo da Vinci's namesake for his study on the human body. It is a new breakthrough in surgery. This system is used for robotically assisted surgery. The surgeon will sit at a console and drive the machine to perform the surgical procedure. The machine assists in allowing the surgical team to perform minimally invasive heart surgeries. Open-heart surgery normally requires a large incision and longer recovery. The robotic system offers an opportunity to perform the same surgery through much smaller openings. The recovery is quicker. There is less blood loss. This procedure offers a great deal of promise.

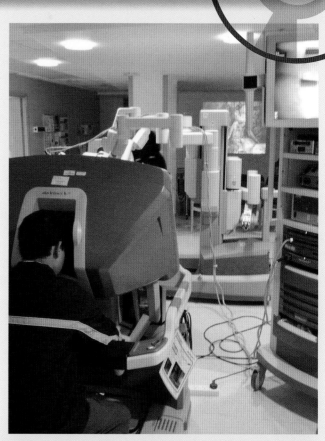

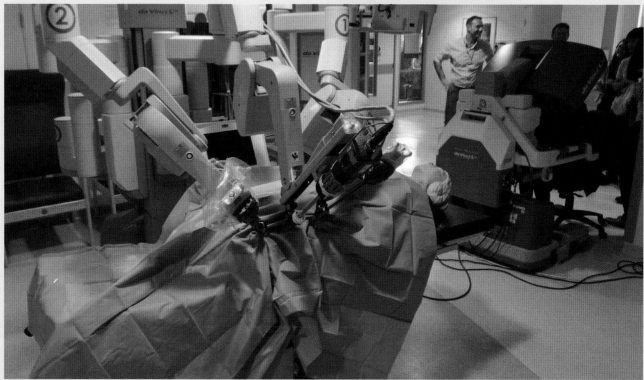

Heart-Lung Machine

The "heart-lung machine," also known as the cardiopulmonary bypass pump, has been a revolutionary invention on the forefront of saving people's lives.

Operating on a moving, beating heart is very challenging. In 1953, Dr. John Gibbon, with his wife Mary, invented the first heart-lung machine after 20 years of development.

Since the Gibbons' invention, the heart-lung machine has improved a great deal. The machine allows blood to bypass (go around) the heart while the surgeons perform delicate surgery. The machine is attached to the patient's large veins that feed into the heart. The blood is re-routed to the heart-lung machine, where oxygen is added. It is pumped back to the body at the large arteries leaving the heart. The heart can be stopped for many hours to perform complicated surgeries.

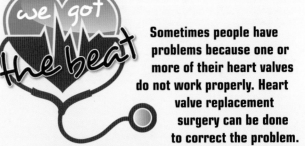

we got the beat

Sometimes people have problems because one or more of their heart valves do not work properly. Heart valve replacement surgery can be done to correct the problem. Patients are given either a manufactured valve or one that has been donated. A lot of people wait each year for various types of organ donations.

Heart-lung machines are very beneficial during certain heart-related surgeries, as shown below. It temporarily takes the place of the heart and lungs for the patient. Doctors have to be careful not to use it for more than 6 to 10 hours.

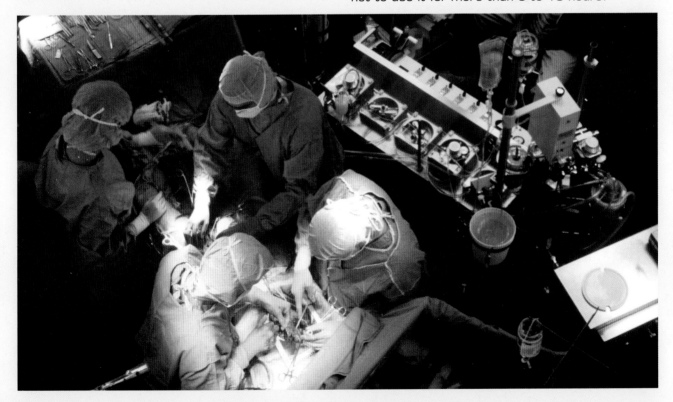

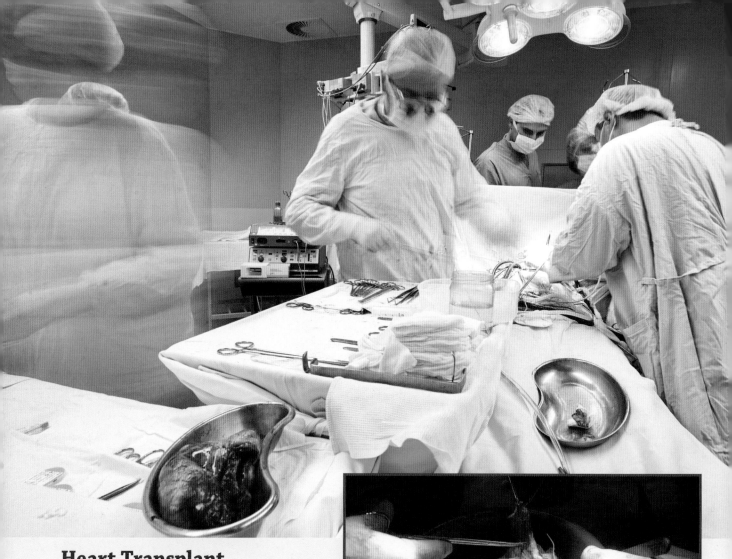

Heart Transplant

God has created our wondrous machine known as our body. Nothing that man has designed comes close. We continue to design better machines and medical devices. None has been able to perform at the level, the duration, or with the precision of God's machines. Organ transplantation has offered many a new lease on life. Sometimes organs begin to fail before the rest of the body. Failures in organs can be due to birth defects, trauma, and disease. Replacement of the diseased organ with a healthy donor organ has saved and allowed patients to live longer.

The first successful heart transplant was performed by Dr. Christiaan Bernard in 1967. It is estimated that a total of 5,000 heart transplants are performed worldwide each year, and approximately 2,000 are performed in the United States alone. The youngest heart transplant patient in the United States was little Oliver. He was born with a heart problem seven weeks early. It was a problem that would have been fatal. He underwent a heart transplant at six days of age. Dick Cheyney, former vice president of the United States, is one of the oldest recipients of a "new" heart at the age of 71.

Coronary Angioplasty

The heart has its own circulatory system. The vessels that travel on the surface of the heart supply it with oxygen. These arteries can become blocked with a buildup of substances called plaque. These plugs can be composed of things like cholesterol and clotted red blood cells. These blocks can happen slowly or suddenly. An artery can become completely blocked, and a heart attack can occur.

Angioplasty can come to the rescue. Angioplasty is a procedure that can open the blocked artery and restore the blood supply. A small, thin tube with a deflated balloon is threaded through an artery in the arm or thigh, and it is floated up to the heart to the location of the blockage.

❶ The small tube is threaded into the blockage.

❷ Once within the blockage, the small balloon is inflated. This pushes the plaque and flattens it to the walls of the artery to allow the blood to flow. In addition to the balloon on the end, a wire stent can be placed over the balloon. When the balloon is inflated, the stent also expands.

❸ The stent is left in place like the scaffolding in a building.

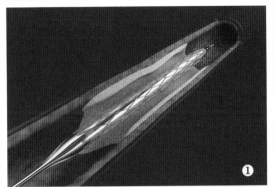

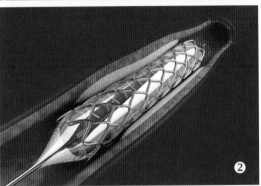

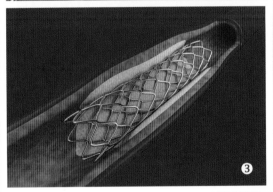

Oliver's surgery was done after his birth, and he is doing well now. But surgeons can also perform heart surgeries on babies still in the womb. There is window of time between 18 and 30 weeks when a variety of surgical procedures can normally be done.

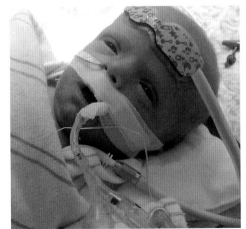

57

Being "heart" healthy seems to be on everyone's minds these days. There are new exercise gadgets and new diets promising good health. It is sometimes hard to discern which of these things will work best for you. There are some foolproof measures that you can do to take good care of your heart.

According to National Geographic, the resting rate of Miguel Indurain, a five-time winner of the famous bike race Tour de France, was once recorded at 28 beats per minute!

Get Moving!

Exercise works your heart muscle. When you engage in heart-pumping exercise, your muscles demand more blood to keep up with its demands for oxygen. There is an increased blood return to your heart. The heart muscle strengthens, and the left ventricle adapts and becomes more efficient. It will be able to eject more blood per minute per beat at work and at rest. Exercise helps with weight loss or maintaining a healthy weight. A normal resting heart rate for most adults is in a range of 60–100 beats per minute. Highly trained athletes can have heart rates as low as 40 beats per minute at rest.

Be Colorful!

Have you ever heard the expression "Eat a Rainbow"? What exactly does that mean? The whole rainbow thing is referring to placing a colorful variety of food on your plate when you eat. Eat your fruits and veggies. No, deep-fried French fries do not count. Eating fruits and vegetables is a great way to put money away in your health bank account.

God has infused fruits and vegetables with antioxidants. Antioxidants are helpful in protecting blood vessels and arteries from the damage that high cholesterol, sugar, and high starchy fatty foods can do. Eating a variety of colors gives you a variety of good stuff for your heart and body. Can you think of good healthy foods that are red, orange/yellow, purple/blue, green, white, and brown? Here are some, see if you can think of more.

- Red: tomatoes, raspberries

- Orange/yellow: squash, carrots

- Purple/blue: blueberries, eggplant

- Green: green peas, kiwi

- White: banana, pear

- Brown: lentils, almonds

Expand Your Universe

Many kids only like starchy carbohydrates like sugary cereals, white hot dog buns, and buttery crackers. Grains like whole grain breads, cereals, and pasta are good in a diet. How about expanding your universe by trading out some of that pasta and bread for a starchy vegetable? You can add corn to a tossed salad. Quinoa is a great intact whole grain. Beans and lentils make a wonderful addition to a diet.

God is our Alpha Omega:
Let's Add a Bit More Omega

Fish like salmon, tuna, and herring are types of oily fish that are rich in omega-3 fatty acids. These types of omega-3 rich foods have been shown to decrease blood pressure, protect the heart, help joints in your body, and decrease unhealthy fat in your blood. Eating this type of fish once a week has its benefits.

59

Why do some people pass out at the sight of blood?

Some people feel queasy at the sight of blood. I have even seen people pass out at the sight of a needle. They simply can't control this reaction. Fainting may have its roots in a reflex in our brain. The fancy term we doctors use in describing this phenomenon is called "vasovagal syncope." This name is derived from the vagus nerve that originates in the brain stem. In Latin, vagus means "wandering." This is a perfect name for a nerve that has many branches. One of the branches runs to the heart.

Intense emotion can activate the vagus nerve. Activation of the vagus nerve in a fainting episode causes a drop in the heart rate. It causes blood vessels to dilate, become wider. This causes a drop in blood pressure. This may be a protective reflex. If you lived in ancient times and you encountered something that could rip off your arm, a fainting response might be a good way to slow down the bleeding. You would look dead, and the animal may lose interest and walk away.

Intense emotion does not have to be unpleasant. Some people faint with intense emotional joy. Case in point — back in the 1964 when the Beatles, a rock group from Liverpool, England, came to the United States. Beatlemania was at its peak. Teenage girls would flock just to get a look at them. Young girls were passing out just at the sight of the members of the rock band.

Why do I sometimes become light-headed when I stand up fast?
Why do some people pass out after standing for long periods of time?

The veins in your legs have valves, which help to keep blood from flowing backward. The contraction of the muscles in your legs, through movement, helps the blood return to your heart. The muscles squeeze the veins. When you stand for prolonged periods without moving, the blood pools in your legs and the blood return to your heart is decreased. This also means the blood flow to your brain is less. Your body responds by having you take a brief "rest." You pass out. This places you in a horizontal position. This increases the blood return to the heart. Your body is happy, and unconsciousness is of a short duration. This is a protective response.

Does living at high altitudes like the mountains of Colorado have an effect on your body?

The Olympic Training Center is located in Colorado Springs, Colorado. This was chosen as the site for training high-level athletes due to its high altitude. This has been thought to improve training performance. The oxygen content of air at high altitudes is less. If you are from areas close to sea level elevation, your body will need to adapt to this high elevation. It takes approximately, on average, 3 to 5 days to adapt to a higher altitude. The bone marrow goes into high gear. It increases red blood cell production to assist with the need for additional oxygen demands of the body. A person whose body has adapted to living at high altitudes may have 30 to 50 percent more red blood cells than those who live at sea level.

What effect do chest compressions have in CPR?

CPR stands for Cardiopulmonary Resuscitation. It is an emergency procedure that a healthcare worker or Good Samaritan can perform in the event that a person's heart or breathing stops. Chest compressions help to keep the blood circulating in an effort to continue the flow of blood and oxygen to the vital organs. The healthcare worker places his or her hands one on top of the other. The hands are placed on the sternum (breastbone). Force on the sternum, pressing it approximately two inches down, compresses the heart between the hard sternum and backbone. This pushes the blood out of the heart. When the person allows the chest to recoil, blood returns to the heart. The cycle is repeated. This can be life-saving in an emergency.

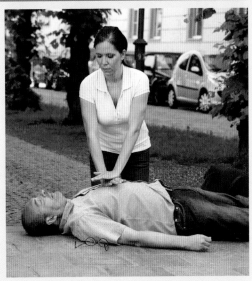

What does it mean when a blood vessel hardens?

Hardening of the arteries is called arteriosclerosis. The arteries become narrowed because fats become loaded on the inside walls. This is called plaque. This plaque grows and hardens. The plaque may even block the artery. This reduces the blood supply to areas of the body like the heart, kidneys, and other organs.

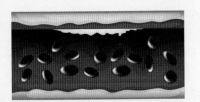 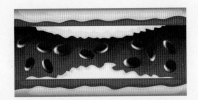 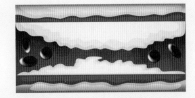

What causes a bruise?

A bruise is caused by rupture of small blood vessels under the skin. When you slip and hit your shin on the step, the impact on your skin causes injury to the underlying vessels. Bleeding occurs under the skin, and it becomes painted with a "beautiful" rainbow of colors.

The Bruise Chart

Day 1		Red, swelling
Days 2–5		Swelling decreases, blue, black, and deep purple, RBCs begin to decay
Days 5–9		Bruise turns green to yellow, WBCs clean up the mess and dispose of decaying RBCs
10+ Days		Light brown, gets lighter and lighter

What is a heart murmur?

We describe the sounds of the heart as "lub dub." You can hear many sounds when you listen to the body with a stethoscope. Sometimes when listening to the heart, you can hear other sounds like a murmur. A heart murmur is the additional sound that can be heard with a beating. It sounds like a whooshing or swishing noise. It is a sound caused by the turbulence of the blood rushing through a valve or an abnormal opening in the heart. It can be a normal sound or abnormal sound. A normal murmur is an innocent murmur heard in some children. This murmur disappears in adulthood.

Conclusion

So glad you joined up with me in awe of God's handiwork on our journey through *The Complex Circulatory System*. I don't tire talking about this wondrous creation inside you and me. As we learned, the circulatory system is indeed a vast expanse with a network of passages that stretch for 60,000 miles. There are between 20-30 trillion red blood cells in your entire body! Lets look at these numbers from another way. One million seconds is about 11.5 days. One billion seconds is about 32 years and ….wait for it….one trillion seconds is equal to approximately 32,000 years! Mind blowing. I struggle to grasp even how much 20-30 trillion must be.

How in the world does God do it? All of this is packed in such small packages. This brings to mind the Psalms in the Bible. The Psalms are wonderful expressions of worship. In Psalm 9:1 it states, "I will praise you, O LORD, with all my heart; I will tell of all your wonders." Learning and talking about science is one of many ways to tell of God's wonders. The only object of praise when we gaze at His wonderment is our heavenly Father. Continue to wonder. Continue to praise Him. Continue to tell of His wonders.

I AM wonderfully made!

Blessed are the pure in heart, for they shall see God (Matthew 5:8).

63

Thumbs Up

In ancient times, it was believed that putting blood on the right ear lobe, right thumb, and right big toe symbolically cleansed every part of a person's life. Blood on the thumb was to atone for the bad things one did. Blood on the toe was to atone for the places one went that were not God-honoring. Blood on the ear was to cover for the bad things one heard and thought.

Sleep Tight, Don't Let the Bedbugs Bite

When I was a little girl, my mother would always say to me after kissing me goodnight, "Sleep tight, don't let the bedbugs bite." I always felt warm and would slip off to sleep contently. I had no idea what that old saying meant.

This expression takes its origins back in the 1800s. Mattresses back then were made of items like straw, leaves, pine needles, or other organic type materials. The problem with beds such as these was that they were a haven for rats, mice, and bedbugs! Yikes! Bedbugs are "charming" little pests. They are insects that love to feast on the blood of animals and people. They do not fly. These little critters sure are fast. They hang out on bedding, near beds, and in walls.

Blood Squirters

"Horned toads" are really horned lizards. Many people think these lizards look like frogs because their bodies are round. They eat a diet rich in harvester ants, which has venom for protection. Horned lizards have a very effective and strange way of defending themselves from predators, like coyotes, foxes, and dogs. When threatened, they actually squirt blood from their eyes. The canines hate this. It is not known why this discourages the predators so much. One theory is that perhaps some of the chemicals from the lizard's diet of harvester ants is excreted with the blood squirt.

Bedbug

Heart Pumping
The heart pumps with such enormous pressure. It is capable of squirting blood up to 9 meters high! (That is 29½ feet.)

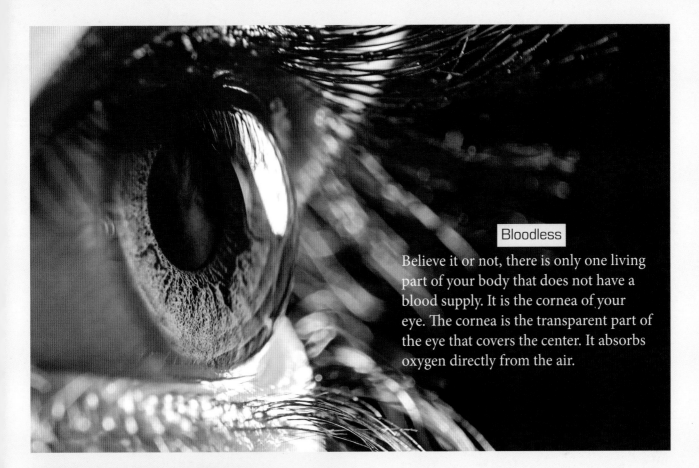

Bloodless

Believe it or not, there is only one living part of your body that does not have a blood supply. It is the cornea of your eye. The cornea is the transparent part of the eye that covers the center. It absorbs oxygen directly from the air.

Feeling Lousy?

Another critter that feasts on blood is the head louse. The head louse (one is a louse; more are called lice) brings its terror by infesting and clinging to the hair of its prey. They are tiny, wingless insects that tend to love little kids. Head lice are spread by sharing hats and combs of someone infected with these little guys. They lay their eggs, called nits, close to the scalp and have easy access to a quick meal.

Hefty Appetite

A typical leech can consume ten times his weight at meal time.

65

You've Got to Be Kidding

What did Mother bat say to her daughter in the morning:	Hurry up and eat your breakfast before it clots.
What is Dracula's favorite ice cream flavor?	Veinilla.
Patient: Doctor, Doctor, I keep thinking I am a mosquito.	Doctor: What a sucker!
Did you hear about the vampire comedian?	He specialized in biting satire.
What is Dracula's favorite fruit?	Necktarines.
What is Dracula's car called?	A Blood Mobile.
Why did the young bat follow his father's profession?	Because it was in his blood.
What's a vampire's favorite dog?	A bloodhound.
Where did they put Dracula when he was arrested?	In a red blood cell.
Why should you never warm up to a snake?	Because they are cold-blooded.
Why did the mosquito go to the dentist?	To improve his bite.
In what do vampires cross the sea?	Blood vessels.
What has antlers and sucks blood?	A moose-quito!
Why are mosquitos religious?	Because they prey on you.

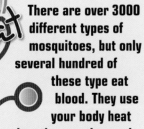

we got the beat

There are over 3000 different types of mosquitoes, but only several hundred of these type eat blood. They use your body heat to locate you when they need a meal. Some mosquitoes bite during the day while other types only bite at night!

Idioms: An idiom is an expression in which the words used mean something different than what they usually mean. Let's play a new game called "Fun with Idioms." You will find heart and blood idioms below. See if you can guess what they mean. See if you can stump your friends and family.

Expression	Meaning
Bleeding heart	A person considered overly emotional about political and other issues
Heart of gold	A very kind and good-natured person
Eat your heart out	Declaring, jokingly or boastfully, that someone is better than someone else
Be all heart	To be kind and generous
Faint of heart	Someone is squeamish, has an upset stomach for something that is unpleasant
Have heart in one's mouth	To feel strongly emotional about someone or something
Warm the cockles of one's heart	To give one a good warm feeling (cockles = chambers of the heart)
Wear one's heart on their sleeve	To display one's emotions openly
Give someone heart failure	To frighten someone
Heart sinks	Feel sad or worried
Half-hearted	Without energy or enthusiasm
Enshrine someone in one's heart	To keep someone's memory alive
Bad blood	Unpleasant feeling, or having a dislike for another person
Be after blood	Actively pursuing someone in order to punish them
Flesh and blood	One of your relatives
Blood in the water	Exposure of a competitive weakness in an opponent that makes the other increasingly aggressive, like sharks on the attack when blood is in the water
Blood is thicker than water	People who are related have stronger feeling to each other than to nonfamily members
Blood is up	Angry
Blood run cold	To be very frightened
Blue blood	A person of royal lineage or wealthy ancestry
Burst a blood vessel	To exert a great deal of effort doing something
Curdle blood	To frighten someone severely
New blood	A new person
Too rich for my blood	Too expensive for one's budget, or too high in fat to eat

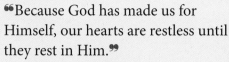

"The best and most beautiful things in the world cannot be seen or even touched — they must be felt with the heart."
—*Helen Keller*

"Sometimes the heart sees what is invisible to the eye."
—*H. Jackson Brown, Jr.*

"The greatest test of courage on earth is to bear defeat without losing heart."
Robert Green Ingersoll

"There is no charm equal to tenderness of heart."
—*Jane Austen*

"Have a heart that never hardens, and a temper that never tires, and a touch that never hurts."
—*Charles Dickens*

"Only God can perform a spiritual heart transplant."
—*Woodrow Kroll*

"Because God has made us for Himself, our hearts are restless until they rest in Him."
—*Augustine of Hippo*

"I love the man that can smile in trouble, that can gather strength from distress, and grow brave by reflection. 'Tis the business of little minds to shrink, but he whose heart is firm, and whose conscience approves his conduct, will pursue his principles unto death."
—*Thomas Paine*

"Wise leaders should have known that the human heart cannot exist in a vacuum. If Christians are forbidden to enjoy the wine of the Spirit they will turn to the wine of the flesh. . . . Christ died for our hearts and the Holy Spirit wants to come and satisfy them."
—*A. W. Tozer*

"Faith is knowledge within the heart, beyond the reach of proof."
—*Khalil Gibran*

5 million patients in the U.S. need blood every year

Every 2 seconds someone needs a blood transfusion

1 pint of blood can save up to 3 lives

"There is a God-shaped vacuum in the heart of every man which cannot be filled by any created thing, but only by God, the Creator, made known through Jesus."
—*Blaise Pascal*

"Grant that I may not pray alone with the mouth; help me that I may pray from the depths of my heart."
—*Martin Luther*

You will sometimes see vans for blood donations in your area. Close to 80% of blood donations that the American Red Cross receives come from these mobile collection sites. You have to meet age and health requirements before you can become a blood donor. According to the American Red Cross, every two seconds someone in the United States will need a blood donation, and around 15.7 million blood donations are collected each year. Donors are vital because blood cannot be created or manufactured.

Less than 38% of the population is eligible to give blood

Blood cannot be manufactured; it can only come from donors

HONORARY donor

Donors can give blood every 56 days

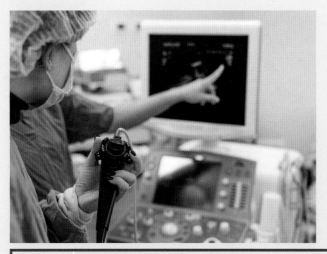
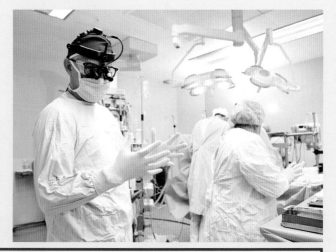

Medical careers can include a lot of different kinds of jobs, including many focused on the heart and circulatory system. Here are just a few:

Biomedical Equipment Technicians	Works in healthcare settings, install, inspect, maintain, repair, modify, and design medical equipment. For example, a perfusionist would operate and manage the heart-lung machine during surgery.
Cardiovascular Technicians	Assist doctors in diagnosing and treating heart and blood vessel problems. They can assist during heart surgery or procedures
Diagnostic Medical Sonographers	Use very specialized equipment that constructs images of the structures in the body that aid doctors in making decisions and diagnosis of problems. They use a machine called an ultrasound. Ultrasound sends sound waves in the body that are painless to the patient. These sound waves bounce off the internal organs. The sound waves are analyzed by a computer and displayed on a screen.
Phlebotomists	People trained to draw blood from a patient for clinical or medical testing, transfusions, donations, or research.
Cardiologist	A doctor that specializes in the care of the heart and blood vessels. There are even pediatric cardiologists. They take care of kids' heart issues.
Cardiovascular Surgeon	Doctors who operate on heart and blood vessels. They repair damage caused by diseases or disorders of the cardiovascular system.
Cardiovascular Rehabilitation Specialist	This specialists work with people who are recovering from heart surgery or people who have heart and lung problems. They educate and design exercise programs to strengthen and improve the health of their patients.

Heart Disease Factors

You can make important choices that help keep your heart healthy! Here are a list of things that can play a role in whether you are at risk for heart disease when you become an adult.

Age		Heart disease can occur at any age, but usually affects people as they get older.	Obesity		Being overweight can lead to high blood pressure and diabetes.
Gender		Men have a higher risk of heart disease than women at any age.	Family History		A risk of heart disease can be inherited from your biological parents.
Tobacco		The chemicals in it hurt the heart, blood cells, and lungs.	Blood Pressure		If it is too high, it can damage blood vessels, making them clogged or weak.
Physical Inactivity		Your heart is a muscle. Thirty minutes a day, five days a week make it stronger.	Diabetes		This impacts insulin levels so your body can't create the fuel it needs.
Alcohol		Drinking raises blood pressure and creates unhealthy fat levels in the blood.	Cholesterol		Too much of it can clog or block your arteries.
Unhealthy Diet		Too much salt, fat, or sugar keeps your body from working at its best.	Stress		This can cause your blood pressure to be too high to be healthy.

Additional Bible Verses on Heart and Blood

Scripture in this section is from the English Standard Version (ESV)

HEART

Jeremiah 17:10	I the Lord search the heart and test the mind, to give every man according to his ways, according to the fruit of his deeds.
Matthew 5:8	Blessed are the pure in heart, for they shall see God.
Hebrews 4:12	For the word of God is living and active, sharper than any two-edged sword, piercing to the division of soul and of spirit, of joints and of marrow, and discerning the thoughts and intentions of the heart.
Proverbs 3:5–6	Trust in the Lord with all your heart, and do not lean on your own understanding. In all your ways acknowledge him, and he will make straight your paths.
Psalm 34:18	The Lord is near to the brokenhearted and saves the crushed in spirit.
James 4:8	Draw near to God, and he will draw near to you. Cleanse your hands, you sinners, and purify your hearts, you double-minded
1 Samuel 16:7	But the Lord said to Samuel, "Do not look on his appearance or on the height of his stature, because I have rejected him. For the Lord sees not as man sees: man looks on the outward appearance, but the Lord looks on the heart"
1 Timothy 1:5	The aim of our charge is love that issues from a pure heart and a good conscience and a sincere faith
Psalm 26:2	Prove me, O Lord, and try me; test my heart and my mind
2 Timothy 2:22.	So flee youthful passions and pursue righteousness, faith, love, and peace, along with those who call on the Lord from a pure heart
Hebrews 10:22	Let us draw near with a true heart in full assurance of faith, with our hearts sprinkled clean from an evil conscience and our bodies washed with pure water
1 Thessalonians 2:4	But just as we have been approved by God to be entrusted with the gospel, so we speak, not to please man, but to please God who tests our hearts
Psalm 119:10	With my whole heart I seek you; let me not wander from your commandments!
Proverbs 16:1	The plans of the heart belong to man, but the answer of the tongue is from the Lord
Matthew 11:29	Take my yoke upon you, and learn from me, for I am gentle and lowly in heart, and you will find rest for your souls

HEART	Luke 16:15	And he said to them, "You are those who justify yourselves before men, but God knows your hearts. For what is exalted among men is an abomination in the sight of God
	Proverbs 22:11	He who loves purity of heart, and whose speech is gracious, will have the king as his friend
	Proverbs 6:18	. . . a heart that devises wicked plans, feet that make haste to run to evil
	Ezekiel 11:19–21	And I will give them one heart, and a new spirit I will put within them. I will remove the heart of stone from their flesh and give them a heart of flesh, that they may walk in my statutes and keep my rules and obey them. And they shall be my people, and I will be their God. But as for those whose heart goes after their detestable things and their abominations, I will bring their deeds upon their own heads, declares the Lord God
	Proverbs 17:3	The crucible is for silver, and the furnace is for gold, and the Lord tests hearts
	Proverbs 14:30	A tranquil heart gives life to the flesh, but envy makes the bones rot
	Psalm 84:2	My soul longs, yes, faints for the courts of the Lord; my heart and flesh sing for joy to the living God
	Ephesians 3:14–20	For this reason I bow my knees before the Father, from whom every family in heaven and on earth is named, that according to the riches of his glory he may grant you to be strengthened with power through his Spirit in your inner being, so that Christ may dwell in your hearts through faith — that you, being rooted and grounded in love, may have strength to comprehend with all the saints what is the breadth and length and height and depth
	Psalm 119:11	I have stored up your word in my heart, that I might not sin against you
BLOOD	1 John 5:6	This is the one who came by water and blood — Jesus Christ; not by the water only but by the water and the blood. And the Spirit is the one who testifies, because the Spirit is the truth
	1 John 1:7	But if we walk in the light, as he is in the light, we have fellowship with one another, and the blood of Jesus his Son cleanses us from all sin
	Romans 5:9	Since, therefore, we have now been justified by his blood, much more shall we be saved by him from wrath of God
	1 Peter 1:1–2	To those…according to the foreknowledge of God the Father, in the sanctification of the Spirit, for obedience to Jesus Christ and for sprinkling with his blood: may grace and peace be multiplied to you
	Matthew 26:28	… for this is my blood of the covenant, which is poured out for many for the forgiveness of sins

Websites

www.brainyquote.com/quotes/keywords/heart.html#rimDCK-8RAdtAym4U.99.

www.goodreads.com/quotes/tag/heart.

www.ncbi.nlm.nih.gov/pmc/articles/PMC3573364/?report=printable, "The Air of History (Part II) Medicine in the Middle Ages," Rachel Hajar, M.D., Heart Views, 2012 Oct–Dec; 13(4): 158–162.

www.earlyamerica.com/early-america-review/volume-9/washingtons-death/.

www.thelancet.com/lancet/about.

www.davincisurgery.com/.

www.icr.org/article/evolution-marlaria

Books

Adler, Robert E. *Medical Firsts: From Hippocrates to the Human Genome.* Hoboken, NJ: John Wiley and Sons, 2004.

Artell, Mike. *Backyard Bloodsuckers: Questions, Facts and Tongue Twisters About Creepy, Crawly Creatures.* Parsippany, NJ: Good Year Books, 2000.

Barnhill, Kelly Regan. *The Bloody Book of Blood.* Mankato, MN: Edge Books/Capstone, 2010.

"blood"— McGraw-Hill's Dictionary of American Slang and Colloquial Expressions. 2006. McGraw-Hill Companies, Inc. 27 Aug. 2015, http://idioms.thefreedictionary.com/blood.

Bragg, Georgia. *How They Croaked: The Awful Ends of the Awfully Famous.* New York, NY: Bloomsbury Publishing, 2011.

Brynie, Faith Hickman. *101 Questions About Blood and Circulation with Answers Straight From the Heart.* Brookfield, CT: Millbrook Press, 2001.

Childress, Kim. *Wacky Bible Gross Outs.* Grand Rapids, MI: Zonderkidz, 2014.

Claybourne, Anna. *100 Most Disgusting Things on the Planet.* New York, NY: Scholastic, 2010.

De La Bedoyere, *Camilla. Ripley's Human Body: Believe it or Not!* Bromall, PA: Mason Crest, 2011.

Dendy, Leslie, and Mel Boring. *Guinea Pig Scientists.* New York, NY: Henry Holt and Company, 2005.

DiConsiglio, John. *Blood Suckers! Deadly Mosquito Bites.* New York, NY: Franklin Watts, 2008.

Ditkoff, Beth Ann, Andrea Ditkoff, and Julia Ditkoff. *Why Don't Your Eyelashes Grow? Curious Questions Kids Ask About the Human Body.* New York, NY: Penguin Group, 2008.

Ferguson Books. *Careers in Focus: Medical Technicians and Technologists.* New York, NY: Infobase Publishing, 2009.

Fradin, Dennis. *Medicine: Yesterday, Today and Tomorrow.* Chicago, IL: Children's Press, 1989.

Gleason, Carrie. *Feasting Bedbugs, Mice, and Ticks.* New York, NY: Crabtree Publishing, 2011.

Hollar, Sherman. *Pioneers in Medicine: From the Classical World to Today.* New York, NY: Encyclopedia Britannica, 2013.

Kalman, Bobbie. *Early Health and Medicine.* New York, NY: Crabtree Publishing, 1991.

Kyi, Tanya Lloyd. *50 Body Questions: A Book That Spills Its Guts.* Buffalo, NY: Annick Press, 2014.

Kyi, Tanya Lloyd. *Seeing Red: The True Story of Blood.* Buffalo, NY: Annick Press, 2012.

Kruszelnicki, Karl. Munching Maggots, *Noah's Flood and TV Heart Attacks and Other Cataclysmic Science Moments.* New York, NY: John Wiley and Sons, 2000.

Law, Kristi. *Clot and Scab: Gross Stuff About Your Scrapes, Bumps and Bruises.* Minneapolis, MN: Millbrook Press, 2010.

Lew, Kristi. Bat Spit, *Maggots, and Other Amazing Medical Wonders.* Mankato, MN: Capstone, 2011.

Markle, Sandra. *Faulty Hearts: True Survival Stories.* Minneapolis, MN: Lerner Publishing, 2011.

Masoff, Joy. *Oh Yikes! History's Grossest Wackiest Moments.* New York, NY: Workman Publishing, 2006.

Masoff, Joy. *Oh Yuck! The Encyclopedia of Everything Nasty.* New York, NY: Workman Publishing, 2000.

Martini, Federic, H., and Kathleen Welch. *Clinical Issues in Anatomy.* San Francisco, CA: Pearson Education, 2006.

Moore, Keith, and T.V.N. Persaud. *The Developing Human: Clinically Oriented Embryology.* Philadelphia, PA: W.B. Saunders, 2003.

Patton, Kevin T. *Survival Guide for Anatomy and Physiology.* St. Louis, MO: Mosby Inc., 2014.

Pinnock, Dale. *Healing Foods: Prevent or Treat Common Illnesses with Fruits, Vegetables, Herbs, and More.* New York, NY. Skyhorse, 2011.

Rhatigan, Joe. *Ouch!* Watertown, MA: Charlesbridge Publications, 2013.

Rodgers, Kara. *Blood: Physiology and Circulation.* New York, NY: Britannica Educational Publishing, 2011.

Rodgers, Kara. *The Cardiovascular System.* New York, NY: Britannica Educational Publishing, 2011.

Rodgers, Kara. *Medicine and Healers Through History.* New York, NY: Britannica Educational Publishing, 2011.

Rooney, Anne. *The Story of Medicine.* London: Arcturus Publishing, 2009.

Sadler, T.W. *Langman's Medical Embryology.* Philadelphia, PA: Williams and Wilkins, 2006.

Singleton, Glen. *Gross Jokes.* Kingley, Australia: Hinkler Books, 2004.

Strom, Laura Layton. *Dr. Medieval: Medicine in the Middle Ages.* New York, NY: Children's Press, 2008.

Tangerine Press. *More Jokes.* New York, NY: Scholastic, 2005.

Tiner, John Hudson. *Exploring the History of Medicine: From the Ancient Physicians of Pharaoh to Genetic Engineering.* Green Forest, AR: Master Books, 1999.

Winner, Cherie. *Circulating Life: Blood Transfusion from Ancient Superstition to Modern Medicine.* Minneapolis, MN: 21st Century Books, 2007.

Bibliography for Activities in **The Complex Circulatory System**

Aims Education. *From Head to Toe: Respiratory, Circulatory and Skeletal Systems, Book 3.* Fresno, CA: Aims Education Foundation, 1986.

Branzei, Sylvia. *Grossology.* New York, NY: Price Stern Sloan, 2002.

Conway, Lorraine. *Superific Science Series: Book IX. Body Systems.* New York, NY:Good Apple, 1984.

Foster, Michael and Patricia Twohey. *The Human Body.* The Education Center, 2000.

Hixson, B.K. *Cow Eyes, Beef, Hearts and Worms.* Salt Lake City, UT: Wild Goose Company, 1992.

Kalumuck, Karen. *Exploratorium Human Body Explorations: Hands On Investigations of What Makes Us Tick.* San Francisco, CA: Exploratorium, 2003.

Reilly, Kathleen. *The Human Body: Illuminate How the Body Works.* White River Junction, VT: Nomad Press, 2008.

Rhatigan, Joe, Rain Newcomb, and Clay Meyer. *Gross Me Out! 50 Nasty Projects to Disgust Your Friends and Repulse Your Family.* New York, NY: Lark Books, 2004.

Romanek, Trudee. *Mysterious You: Squirt! The Most Interesting Book You'll Read Ever About Blood.* Toronto, ON: Kids Can Press, 2005.

VanCleave, Jance. *Play and Find Out about the Human Body: Easy Experiments for Young Children.* New York, NY: Scholastic, 1998.

Haslam, Andrew, and Liz Wyse. *Body — Make it Work! The Hands-on Approach to Science.* New York, NY: Scholastic, 1997.

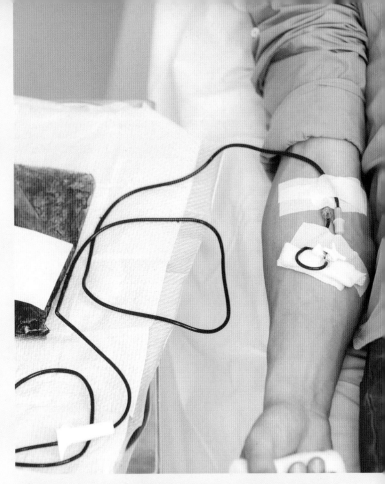

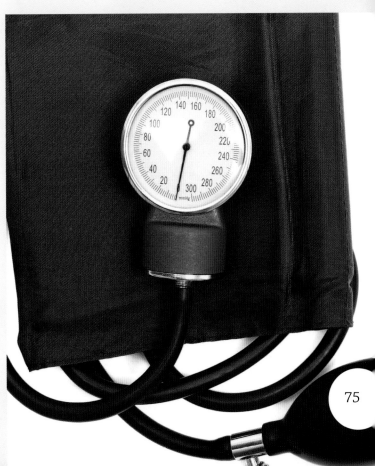

INDEX

Photo credits:

wonders of the HUMAN BODY SERIES

INTRODUCTION TO ANATOMY & PHYSIOLOGY 1

INTRODUCTION TO ANATOMY & PHYSIOLOGY 2

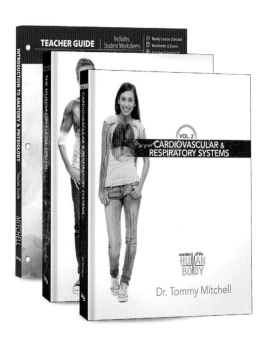

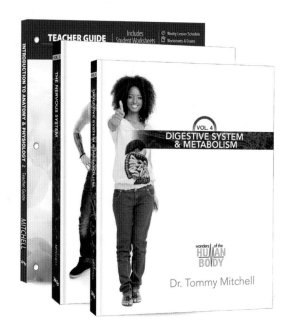

Learn about the musculoskeletal system and the cardio and respiratory systems from the cell level to the systems themselves. There will be no denying that the human body can only be the product of a Master Designer.

3 Book set : 978-0-89051-946-2

Learn about the incredible complexity of the nervous system, where your student will realize that their bodies cannot be the result of chemical accidents occurring over millions of years. They will then study the function of digestion, a highly complex system created by God to transform food into fuel for our energy, something called metabolism, and to take waste from the body. The human body is the greatest creation of an all-knowing Master Designer!

3 Book set : 978-1-68344-145-8

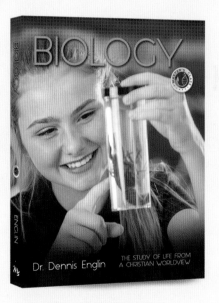

MasterBooks® CURRICULUM

> ❝ **THANKS TO MASTER BOOKS, OUR YEAR IS GOING SO SMOOTHLY!**
> — SHAINA ❞

Made for "Real World" Homeschooling

FAITH-BUILDING

We ensure that a biblical worldview is integral to all of our curriculum. We start with the Bible as our standard and build our courses from there. We strive to demonstrate biblical teachings and truth in all subjects.

TRUSTED

We've been publishing quality Christian books for over 40 years. We publish best-selling Christian authors like Henry Morris, Ken Ham, and Ray Comfort.

EFFECTIVE

We use experienced educators to create our curriculum for real-world use. We don't just teach knowledge by itself. We also teach how to apply and use that knowledge.

ENGAGING

We make our curriculum fun and inspire a joy for learning. We go beyond rote memorization by emphasizing hands-on activities and real-world application.

PRACTICAL

We design our curriculum to be so easy that you can open the box and start homeschooling. We provide easy-to-use schedules and pre-planned lessons that make education easy for busy homeschooling families.

FLEXIBLE

We create our material to be readily adaptable to any homeschool program. We know that one size does not fit all and that homeschooling requires materials that can be customized for your family's wants and needs.

VISIT **MASTERBOOKS**.COM — *Where Faith Grows!* — TO SEE OUR FULL LINE OF FAITH-BUILDING CURRICULUM OR CALL 800-999-3777.